Continuing Professional Development in the Lifelong Learning Sector

Continuing Professional Development in the Lifelong Learning Sector

Peter Scales
Jo Pickering
Lynn Senior
Kath Headley
Patsy Garner
Helen Boulton

 Open University Press

Open University Press
McGraw-Hill Education
McGraw-Hill House
Shoppenhangers Road
Maidenhead
Berkshire
England
SL6 2QL

email: enquiries@openup.co.uk
world wide web: www.openup.co.uk

and
Two Penn Plaza, New York, NY 10121-2289, USA

First published 2011

A catalogue record of this book is available from the British Library

ISBN-13: 978 0 335 23817 0 (pb) / 978 0 335 23818 7 (hb)
ISBN-10: 0335 238173 (pb) / 0335 23818 1 (hb)

Library of Congress Cataloging-in-Publication Data
CIP data has been applied for

Typeset by Aptara Inc., India
Printed in the UK by Bell & Bain Ltd, Glasgow

Fictitous names of companies, products, people, characters and/or data that may be used herein (in case studies or in examples) are not intended to represent any real individual, company, product or event.

The *McGraw·Hill* Companies

This book, with love and laughs, is for Vanessa; Julian; John; Carole; Sandy;
Shula and little Barry (Pete)

To Dave (Helen)

To Phil, Fleur and Chloe, who always have to put up with my madcap schemes (Jo)

Thank you Allan, Thomas and Jon for your everlasting strength and fortitude
that has enabled me to take time to go bouldering, and work in a team
to score a goal . . . a winner! (Kath)

To my wonderful husband and family for all their support and encouragement (Patsy)

To Paul and my family for their love and support (Lynn)

Contents

Acknowledgements   *viii*
Author profiles   *ix*
List of acronyms and abbreviations   *xi*

Introduction   1

1 CPD in the lifelong learning sector   3

2 Being a professional in the lifelong learning sector   17

3 The reflective practitioner   33

4 The CPD process   53

5 CPD for the new teacher   72

6 CPD for teaching and learning   86

7 Subject-specific CPD   113

8 The teacher as researcher   133

Bibliography   *148*
Index   *155*

Acknowledgements

The authors and publishers wish to thank Gillian Forrester of Gateshead College and Shiela Kearney, Head of Research at LSIS for permission to use the article from *Inside Evidence*, Spring 2010; Charles Dietz for permission to use the Comberton Village College case study from *Curriculum Briefing* Vol. 4, No. 2; Ann Bullock and Loughborough College for the interviews and permission to produce a case study, and Jackie Hall for permission to reproduce her action research report.

We would also like to thank our colleagues at the University of Derby, Peter Tunnicliffe and Kelly Briddon for their stalwart support, advice and suggestions. Also Vanessa Scales for her HR advice and expertise.

Our sincere thanks go to Fiona Richman and Stephanie Frosch of McGraw-Hill for their support and patience. Thanks also to our copy editor, Maureen Cox, for her diligence and patience.

Author profiles

Peter Scales is Senior Teaching Fellow in the Faculty of Education, Health and Sciences at the University of Derby. He is a member of the Lifelong Learning Initial Teacher Training team and also of the Postgraduate Certificate in Higher Education for lecturing staff at the University of Derby. He is the author of *Teaching in the Lifelong Learning Sector* (Open University Press, 2008) His recent research was based around employability for graduate students. Prior to his university role Peter had over 20 years experience teaching English, communication and media studies and teacher training at local further education colleges.

Jo Pickering is Head of Subject for Education Studies at the University of Derby with responsibility for Lifelong Learning, Early Years and Education Studies programmes. Prior to her university role Jo had considerable experience as a teacher and manager in further education, schools, adult education and consultancy. Jo has recently completed a secondment with the National College for Leadership of Schools and Children's Services, focusing on middle leadership programmes. Her recent research concentrated on induction and CPD for newly qualified teachers.

Lynn Senior is Assistant Subject Head responsible for Lifelong Learning Initial Teacher Training at the University of Derby. She is also the programme leader for the Postgraduate Certificate in Higher Education. Her current research interests are in the area of 14–19 learning; her book *Hints and Tips for Diploma Teachers* was published by Pearson in May 2010.

Kath Headley is programme leader for the full-time Postgraduate Diploma in Teaching in the Lifelong Learning Sector at the University of Derby. Prior to her university role Kath had considerable experience as a teacher and manager in a further education college. Her research interests are in the development of reflective practice for teachers in the lifelong learning sector.

Patsy Garner coordinates the FE college partnerships for the Certificate and Diploma in Teaching in the Lifelong Learning Sector at the University of Derby. Prior to her university role Patsy had extensive experience as a teacher and manager in a range of further education colleges. Her current research interests include ICT/IT teaching and learning strategies and e-learning opportunities.

Helen Boulton is programme leader for the part-time Diploma in Teaching in the Lifelong Learning Sector at the University of Derby. Prior to her university role she was a teacher trainer at a local further education college. Her research interests include the development of individual learning plans in the lifelong learning sector.

Acronyms and abbreviations

This list contains only the acronyms used in this book. Acronyms and abbreviations are so prevalent in the LLS that you could probably claim 30 hours CPD just from learning them!

The University and College Union (UCU) provides an online *'A-Z of FE and HE'*, a really useful and comprehensive dictionary of acronyms, abbreviations and terminology with links to websites.

ACM	Association of College Managers
AI	Appreciative Inquiry
ALC	Advanced Learning Coach
APL	Accreditation of prior learning
ATLS	Associate Teacher Learning and Skills
Becta	British Educational Communications and Technology Association
BERA	British Educational Research Association
BTEC	Business and Technology Education Council
CETT	Centre(s) for Excellence in Teacher Training
CIPD	Chartered Institute of Personnel and Development
CPD	continuing professional development
CSCL	computer supported collaborative learning
CTLLS	Certificate in Teaching in the Lifelong Learning Sector
DCSF	Department for Children, Schools and Families
DfES	Department for Education and Skills (was replaced by DIUS and DCSF)
DTLLS	Diploma in Teaching in the Lifelong Learning Sector
ERIC	Educational Resources Information Centre
ESOL	English for speakers of other languages
FE	further education
FENTO	Further Education Training Organisation
FESDF	Further Education Staff Development Forum
HE	higher education
HEA	Higher Education Academy
ICT	Information and Communications Technology
IfL	Institute for Learning
IFP	Increased Flexibility Programme
ILM	Institute of Leadership and Management
ILP	Individual (or Initial) Learning Plan

INSET   in-service education and training
IQER   integrated quality and enhancement review
IT   information technology
ITT   initial teacher training
LDD   learning difficulties and disability
LLS   lifelong learning sector
LLUK   Lifelong Learning UK
LSIS   Learning and Skills Improvement Service
NEET   not in education, employment or training
NOSS   national occupational standards
Ofsted   Office for Standards in Education
PBL   problem-based learning
PDJ   Personal Development Journal
PGCE   Postgraduate Certificate in Education
PLTS   personal, learning and thinking skills
PTLLS   Preparing to Teach in the Lifelong Learning Sector
QCA   Qualifications and Curriculum Authority
QCDA   Qualifications and Curriculum Development Agency
QIA   Quality Improvement Agency (now merged with Centre for
         Excellence in Leardership to become the Learning and Skills
         Improvement Service)
QTLS   Qualified Teacher Learning and Skills
SLC   Subject Learning Coach
SSAT   Specialist Schools and Academies Trust
SSC   sector skills council
SVUK   Standards Verification UK
TDA   Teacher Development Agency
TLRP   Teaching and Learning Research Project
UKCES   UK Commission for Employment and Skills
VAKT   visual, auditory, kinaesthetic, tactile

Introduction

The key message of this book is that teachers are best placed to make decisions regarding their own continuing professional development (CPD). Teachers know, or should know, their subjects and their learners' needs within their local context. The Institute for Learning (IfL) CPD model and guidelines provide a real opportunity for teachers to start reclaiming the initiative and to take responsibility for their own learning and development and for organizations and managers to move away from 'sheep-dip' approaches to CPD to personalized learning. If we seriously intend to personalize learning for our students then, surely, the same principle must apply to teachers.

Teachers in the lifelong learning sector (LLS) are encouraged to think of themselves as professionals but people don't become professional or behave professionally just because they are told to. The essential characteristics of professionalism are autonomy, specialist knowledge and responsibility. These are the very characteristics which professionals, not just in education, feel have been increasingly eroded by excessive control from the centre and managerialism. The authors of this book believe that teachers need to be trusted and treated as professionals and that this is a key element in improving teaching and learning. Teachers have a right to be professionals but they also have a responsibility to be professionals. Part of this responsibility is to engage in meaningful CPD which benefits them, their organization and, above all, their learners.

The IfL CPD model is based on the notion of the 'dual professional', that is being a subject specialist but also continually developing their understanding of the theory and practice of teaching and learning. It is important that those currently in the sector and those about to enter it understand the changing nature of teaching and learning and of lifelong learning. The purpose of teaching is learning. For many, however, teaching is still seen as a process of transmission of knowledge from an expert to students and the retention of this knowledge being assessed in some way. Clearly, the role of the subject expert teacher is vital to learning; learners want teachers who 'know their stuff'. Unfortunately, the 'stuff' teachers know goes out of date quite quickly. Consequently teachers will have to become not only subject experts but people who can help learners to learn as well as being lifelong learners themselves. As Wells (1986: 222) says, 'At every level, students must be encouraged actively to take responsibility for their own learning, and this applies as much to teachers as learners as it does to the students they teach' (Wells 1986: 222).

In this rapidly changing context teachers need to become researchers and developers of their own practice and to be engaged in dialogue with their fellow professionals. Teachers will feel at their most professional if they are given the opportunities to understand and explore teaching and learning in their own contexts and trusted to find solutions to problems and to improve their practice. The emphasis on local context is important since no two places of learning are the same; they will have different students and staff from diverse communities with a wide range of needs and experiences.

While teachers at regional and national level can, and should, communicate and share ideas, it is important to remember that solutions cannot be imported from one organization to another and be expected to have the same, or any, effect. We need to be wary of notions of 'best practice' in teaching and learning which can, if we are not careful, come to be the only acceptable practice.

This book also carries messages for managers and executive teams about their role in encouraging CPD and providing the structures in which it can flourish. Continuing professional development applies to everyone in an educational organization – executives; managers; team leaders; teachers and learners. Everyone should be learning in a learning organization.

Who is this book for?

The lifelong learning sector includes further education; adult and community learning; work-based learning; private training providers and offender learning. This book is intended for all of these, and more, including:

- any pre-service or in-service trainee teachers taking courses leading to: Preparing to Teach in the Lifelong Learning Sector (PTLLS); Certificate in Teaching in the Lifelong Learning Sector (CTTLS); Diploma in Teaching in the Lifelong Learning Sector (DTTLS);
- those who have qualified to teach since 2001 who wish to gain Qualified Teacher Learning and Skills (QTLS) or 'brush up' their knowledge and skills;
- teachers in colleges working with 14–16-year-olds;
- teachers in sixth forms and sixth form colleges;
- trainers in private training providers.

How to use this book

Given that the defining characteristics of professionalism are autonomy and knowledge it seems impertinent, as well as unnecessary, to tell you how to use this book. The chapter headings and introductory summaries are quite clear, so begin wherever you want. Chapter 1 sets the scene and makes clear that CPD is a professional responsibility, but also a right for teachers in the sector. Engaging with some of the arguments and debates surrounding CPD introduced in Chapter 1 provides a context for the subsequent chapters and reminds us that CPD is more than just about maintaining one's licence to practice – it is the key to improving teaching and learning.

Terminology

Throughout the book we have used the term 'learner' to include, at least, the following: student, trainee and apprentice. 'Teacher' is used to indicate lecturer, teacher, trainer and tutor.

1 CPD in the lifelong learning sector

> Continuing professional development means maintaining, improving and broadening relevant knowledge and skills in your subject specialism and your teaching so that it has a positive impact on practice and learner experience.
>
> (IfL 2009c: 4)

> The outstanding characteristic of the extended professional is a capacity for autonomous professional self-development through systematic self-study, through the study of the work of other teachers and through the testing of ideas by classroom research procedures.
>
> (Stenhouse 1975: 144)

This chapter is about:

- The 'paradoxes' of CPD
- The changing context of CPD
- CPD and professionalism
- CPD – the role of management
- Learning organizations – the way forward?

The IfL is the professional body which regulates and provides standards for those working in the lifelong learning sector. It also grants teachers a licence to practice. In order to maintain this licence to practice teachers must provide evidence of their CPD, which is sampled and monitored by the Institute. The IfL makes clear in its guidelines that CPD is 'a responsibility for all teachers and employers across the further education sector' (IfL 2009a: 4). Being a professional brings responsibilities but, as Coffield (2008: 24) points out: CPD is a responsibility for all professionals but it is also a right. If 'personalised' learning is the new government aim for all students, then it should apply equally to staff, who have their own learning needs, gaps and aspirations.

This tension between right and responsibility is central to the discussions surrounding CPD in the lifelong learning sector. However, there should be no doubt about the efficacy of professional development and its central role in improving learning. Thompson and William (2007: 2) plainly state that:

> We were led to teacher professional development as the fundamental lever for improving student learning by a growing body of research on the influences on

student learning, which shows that teacher quality trumps virtually all other influences on student achievement.

Paradoxes of CPD

Megginson and Whitaker (2003: 19), writing on CPD for the Chartered Institute of Personnel and Development (CIPD), identify seven dilemmas or 'paradoxes' of CPD in order to explore its complexity. For the current purpose we have chosen six of these as ways of discussing the contested nature of CPD.

Compulsion or voluntarism

This goes to the heart of people's feelings about CPD and its role and purpose. Megginson and Whitaker (2007: 15) note that one of the primary motivations for CIPD members undertaking CPD is 'to avoid losing one's licence to practice', and in this respect they are probably no different from members of other professions. However, observation and anecdotal evidence suggest that teachers in the LLS regularly undertake some form of CPD and, indeed, it may be so embedded in their practice that they don't recognize it as such. It is perhaps more likely to be the case that teachers' reservations are about the value of recording and logging CPD rather than the value of the development activities themselves. However, if we are to be members of a professional organization we have, in common with other professions, to be able to demonstrate our CPD in order to maintain our licence to practice. It is important for teachers, managers and the Institute to continue to develop the most effective methods of recording and logging and emphasize that these are *evidence* of CPD; they are not an end in themselves. Attitudes to CPD will be discussed further in this chapter.

Employer or individual responsibility

Teachers in the lifelong learning sector have become accustomed to 'having things done to them' and being required to comply with a whole raft of documentation and activities, frequently said to be part of their 'professional responsibilities', which they perceive as not directly related to improving learning. While it is a basic tenet that individual teachers have a responsibility to undertake CPD, it should also be accepted that managers, particularly senior managers, have a responsibility to create an ethos which encourages professional development and values it as the most effective way to 'put teaching and learning at the heart of what we do' (DfES 2002). There is a balance to be struck here; colleges and other providers have strategic goals they need to meet, but if teachers are instructed to undertake particular development activities as management dictat, there will be, at best, grudging compliance. If the mission and goals of the organization are communicated to all, teachers should, and can, be trusted to find the best ways to develop teaching and learning within that framework.

Teaching or learning

This paradox reflects debates about student learning. Most people working in education will recognize the need for teachers to be subject specialists and to impart information and knowledge to their learners; we shouldn't characterize didactic practice as 'bad teaching'. Equally, however, there is a growing recognition that students need to become people who can do things with what they are 'given' – to apply; adapt; modify; challenge, even to reject some of it. Part of the teacher's role is to encourage independent lifelong learning. The same is true of CPD. There will be occasions when teachers need specific inputs from experts in order to, for example, understand and use new technology. There are probably very few occasions when all teachers will need, or benefit from, the same input at the same time. The most effective CPD is based around teachers learning, individually and collaboratively, in their own situations and exploring and creating better ways of learning. As we will see later, teachers are best placed to know what they need.

Personal development or organizational learning

Put simply, the answer is probably that both personal and organizational learning are needed for learners, teachers and organizations to succeed and cope with change. The argument is, rightly, put that organizations can't learn; only people can learn. However, if learning is seen as the core activity of the organization then it is more likely that it will be more successful – not just for the learners but also for adapting to and surviving in difficult circumstances. 'Learning organizations' will be considered in more detail later in this chapter.

Values driven or pragmatic development

Most colleges and learning providers have honourable intent and believe that their role is to provide education and encourage learning. Such values are often enshrined in mission statements and marketing information. In reality, these goals are frequently undermined or have to be modified in light of the latest policy shift. Colleges have, in recent years, been seen as the agents of achieving social or economic ends, for example, tackling social exclusion or solving unemployment, and have performed some remarkable reorientations in their structure and practices only for them to rapidly become unsuited to the next policy shift. In this shifting landscape, managers and teachers are often just firefighting and having to adapt and compromise their values and, consequently, professional development becomes subverted into merely training staff to meet the demands of the latest 'big idea'. The values of education are, in essence, quite simple – they're about learning – and should be constant and relatively timeless. If we accept these values and stay with them then we can really concentrate on developing as teachers and subject specialists, indeed, as professionals, rather than having to react to government caprice.

Journey or exploration

The metaphors of a 'journey' or an 'exploration' are useful ways of understanding two contrasting approaches to CPD. In the journey metaphor the destination is known in advance but there may be discussion and negotiation regarding the route, the time allowed and the methods of transport. Many people will want to get there in the shortest possible time; others might want to take the most scenic route even if it costs more and takes longer. In CPD terms, the journey might be towards the achievement of a particular goal, for example, gaining an assessor award or learning how to use a new piece of technology. In such cases the journey is the most appropriate metaphor and specific means for reaching the destination might be identified or prescribed and budgets allocated accordingly. In other cases, the journey approach with preconceived goals and outcomes can be restricting. You might arrive at your destination and soon realize it's not the best place to be and you might have missed several interesting and important diversions along the way. Before this metaphor is stretched to breaking point, let's consider the notion of exploration. Going 'exploring' has connotations of finding things out and the final destination is not necessarily known. Goals for an exploration are wider, looser, sometimes ill defined, but you might end up in a place you didn't know existed which yields great treasures. Continuing professional development developed by teachers in their subject specialism – especially experiments and action research projects – are explorations. The problem is that such explorations may appear to be expensive indulgences by the explorers and managers who will need to weigh the costs with the likely benefits. Explorers and the people who sponsor them have to be prepared for culture shocks and encountering unfamiliar ideas and methods which don't fit in with their existing views and beliefs; these are the real benefits of exploration – if you're not prepared to change, don't take the journey.

CPD – the changing context

As you will discover in Chapter 2, the definition and meanings around 'profession' and 'professionalism' are somewhat fluid. Traditionally, the notion of the 'professional' carried with it some powerful but unspoken associations. These included the idea of 'entry' to the professions being dependent on specialist knowledge and skills, professional autonomy, authority and altruism. Professionalism also implied virtuous behaviour; the much lampooned phrase, 'Trust me, I'm a professional', was probably once said without irony. The professions, and entry to them, were strictly regulated by professional bodies, organized and run by members of that profession; those discovered to have behaved inappropriately were liable to be 'struck off'.

The forces leading to changes in the meanings of professionalism are beyond the scope of this book, but the shifts revolve around the notions of respect and status and a growing tendency to regard professionals as self-serving, exclusive and resistant to change. Gradually professions could no longer be considered fit to make their own rules and to regulate themselves. The tacit principles of the professions came to be seen as vague and archaic and were gradually replaced by 'standards' which codified in detail the values, behaviour, knowledge and skills of the profession. The first manifestation of this in further education was the FENTO Standards, now superseded by the Lifelong Learning UK (LLUK) Professional Standards. The imposition of these standards in the LLS, and the endorsement and maintenance of them by Standards Verification UK (SVUK) is seen by many as symptomatic of increasing control and standardized approaches to teacher training in the sector (see, for example, Avis et al. 2010). Uniform approaches and the introduction of professional standards reinforce a perceived decline in teacher and teacher trainer autonomy, and in the importance of their specialist subject knowledge and expertise.

The professions and many other areas of work, have been since the Conservative government of 1979 and through the New Labour period, profoundly affected by the rise of 'managerialism', an ideology which has at its heart a rejection of the notion of professionialism and is structured by the belief that organizations – whether they be colleges, supermarkets or car manufacturers – have more similarities than they have differences and that their performance can be optimized by the application of generic management theory and skills and an audit culture. Control is the essence of managerialism and 'is underpinned by an ideology which assumes that all aspects of organisational life should be controlled. In other words, that ambiguity can and should be radically reduced and eliminated' (Wallace and Hoyle 2005, in James and Biesta 2007: 135). This control is external through government agencies, funding bodies and inspection bodies, whose influence is then felt by management teams who may feel unable or unwilling to take risks with non-standard 'products' and methods or with things which can't be measured or audited in some way.

Hayes et al. (2007) refer to the 'perverse consequences' of government policies designed to meet a perceived need or deficit but which produce effects that were not intended. They discuss the 'new professionalism' which began in schools with the setting of generic standards for the school workforce, which then rapidly took root in further education (FE):

> This 'new' professionalism has major perverse consequences. It undermines professionalism. . . . if the government is telling you that you must be professional in certain ways, this undermines professionalism. Being 'professional' is not about doing what the government or its regulatory quangos say. Professionalism is necessarily autonomous and is based on personal knowledge and skills alone.
>
> (Hayes et al. 2007: 20)

The formula for 'success' in education, which seems to result from these ideological and political foundations can be expressed quite simply:

- An educational 'product' (examination; qualification) is conceived in a framework of standards and outcomes.
- This educational 'product' takes its place within a national framework of qualifications, vetted by qualification authorities.

- Delivery and teaching methods are recommended, some might say pre-scribed. Examples of 'best practice' are provided.
- Teachers are trained within a framework of national standards and 'preferred' teaching methods are encouraged.
- Educational 'products' are 'delivered' by teachers.
- Provision and delivery are 'quality checked' using 'quality standards'.
- Results are published and praised or criticized accordingly.
- Future funding is predicated on these 'successes'.

The results of success are published and celebrated. Learners should celebrate success and for many of them these successes, demonstrated by qualifications and certificates, will open doors into further and higher education and into work. The question remains, however, whether this process has resulted in lifelong learning and an increasing ability to take responsibility for one's own learning and development.

This conception of learning and education is based very much on the 'delivery' metaphor. Within this metaphorical model is an assumption that educational 'products' have been quality checked and are, therefore, suitable for purpose. Consequently, non-success is seen as failure in the delivery – by teachers, colleges and learning providers – which can then be identified and rectified by inspection bodies.

Browne et al. (2008) consider these changes and discuss their consequences in the context of government concerns about learners leaving education with inadequate functional skills and a perceived lack of skills for economic competitiveness. They state that:

> The policy response to this perceived problem of underachievement was articulated in the words of 'Success for All' (DfES 2002) and communicated in the declared aim to transform teaching and learning. This policy marked a change in focus in its articulation of blame away from the commonly held view that fault laid with learners, to a perception of failure on the part of staff working in the FE sector. This failure was made public in an Ofsted report into the quality of teaching and learning in the sector which identified systemic weaknesses in the sector.
>
> (Browne et al. 2008: 428)

Success for All was a key document and the positive tone of its title was welcome. From this document followed a series of changes which have radically altered the teacher training landscape. *Equipping our Teachers for the Future* (DfES 2004) provided the framework for the reform of initial teacher training, including the recommended structure of the new courses of training; the introduction of LLUK and the new professional standards; the setting up of Centres for Excellence in Teacher Training (CETTs), and developing the work of the Standards Unit.

The machinery for improvement in the LLS now seems to be complete and operational. A key component of this machinery is the notion of a professional workforce. If we take the conception of a 'professional' proposed by the IFL (2009b: 3) as a person who has autonomy, individual expertise and specialist knowledge, to what extent does this conception fit within a context which is still based on external control and regulation? We are presented with another paradox; can the new LLUK professional standards and the IfL obligation to undertake and record CPD give teachers in the LLS a real opportunity to rediscover professionalism or will professionalism only be possible in 'certain ways' which are not necessarily agreed and endorsed by teachers?

Can CPD professionalize the LLS workforce?

The answer, in a nutshell, is no. Continuing professional development on its own does not make a professional but the introduction of the IfL and the requirement for CPD offer some real possibilities for teachers to seize the initiative and take some control of their own CPD and possibly, as a consequence, become more professional. Villeneuve-Smith et al. (2009: 13) suggest that, 'the move to professionalise the workforce changes everything – arguably for the better'.

From 'sheep-dip' to personalized CPD

Those who have been working in the sector for some time, particularly in FE, will be familiar with the 'sheep-dip' approach to staff development in which all teaching staff were 'invited' to attend mass training events, usually at the end of an academic year, which were chosen by others on their behalf. This in-service education and training (INSET) model has the attraction that it is relatively cheap, provides easily auditable evidence of training and causes minimum disruption to the organization's main purpose – teaching and learning. There are, undoubtedly, good examples of effective INSET events, especially to provide an introduction to a major new initiative. Equally, there are probably as many bad examples which, while they may tick some boxes, are not good models of teaching and learning. Villeneuve-Smith et al. (2009: 6) ask:

> Have you ever sat through a badly taught training day on good teaching? Suffered death by PowerPoint on a programme for innovative uses of e-learning? Attended a didactically taught course on active learning? . . . it could be argued that good CPD should practise what it preaches. Why should the sector accept development activities that don't reflect in their delivery what you already know about good teaching and learning?

If personalization, with its acknowledgement of learners as individuals located within specific contexts and with a wide range of needs and ways of learning, is the new mantra in the sector then surely the same should apply to teachers and their CPD. This conception of CPD, based on a professional dialogue about teaching and learning, reflects what the IfL is looking for, indeed, the IfL Review of CPD (IfL 2009c: 11) urges,

1   'a broad interpretation of CPD beyond attendance at courses, workshops or formal study'
     and

2   'a personalised approach to CPD; practitioners leading in their own CPD and using judgement and expertise to develop leading edge practice in teaching and training.'

The IfL CPD guidelines provide a comprehensive list of the kinds of activities which are in line with these principles, including mentoring new colleagues, peer observation and review, and action research.

Personalized CPD, by implication, should mean a move to more teacher autonomy and the recognition that professional teachers, in their specific contexts and subject disciplines, are best placed to recognize problems that need to be solved or to identify opportunities for improvement.

The role of management in encouraging personalized CPD

Since the incorporation of FE colleges in 1993 and the infiltration of managerialism and audit cultures, college managements have changed as a consequence. Anecdotal evidence suggests there are managers and management teams who enjoy the tight control and opportunities for 'macho' management which have been made possible by this environment. It is likely, however, that there as many managers who do not like this environment but feel unable to take risks. Management teams are frequently set seemingly impossible, and contradictory, tasks, such as widening participation while simultaneously raising standards and improving results. Managers may indeed wish to support their staff in being professional and making their own judgements and decisions but fear that such autonomy may lessen the effectiveness and success of delivering educational 'products'. Managers such as these probably know that teachers feel a loss of autonomy and respect but consider these to be lesser problems than the penalties, redundancies and possible takeover or closure which follow a poor inspection or lack of 'success' in measurable terms.

There are several ways in which management teams can encourage personalized CPD; three main approaches will be considered here:

1   providing a structured CPD framework;
2   encouraging collaboration and the development of learning communities;
3   setting the right tone – appreciative inquiry.

Providing a structured CPD framework

The teachers' dream scenario might be one where managers adopt a 'set my people free' approach in which teachers are completely free to manage teaching and learning and associated CPD. This is not going to happen. Given that budgets will remain tight and external control is not likely to disappear soon, CPD needs to be organized within a structured framework, if only to avoid repetition and waste. More importantly development needs to be coordinated and it will have to be in line, as far as possible, with the organization's agreed mission and goals. A key question concerns how and at what level are such goals discussed and agreed: if teachers are to be valued and their professionalism encouraged it would seem appropriate for them to be involved in committees and other bodies which formulate policy and procedures related to teaching, learning and CPD. A strategic approach to CPD needs to be supported, not necessarily led, right from the top. Managers need to signify that CPD is valued as a key driver for improvement, rather than just another policy to be written and signed off.

Encouraging collaboration and the development of learning communities

There is a body of learning theory – social constructivism – which asserts that learners learn best in groups where they can share and develop ideas and contribute to solving problems. The same is true for teachers who, to use a clichéd old phrase, need peers and, possibly, colleagues from different disciplines, to 'bounce ideas off'.

Good teachers are also good learners; their CPD is based on learning. Coffield (2008) suggests two contrasting metaphors of learning which apply equally well to learners and teachers. The first is the *acquisition* metaphor in which learning is seen as gaining ownership of knowledge and skills, endorsed by certificates from examination boards or certificates of attendance at training events. This metaphor employs such key words as 'delivery' and 'transmission'. In contrast the *participation* metaphor, with its associated key words, 'community, identity, meaning, practice, dialogue, co-operation and belonging' (Coffield 2008: 8), suggests that learning results from participation in communities of practice which learn, share, develop and communicate within a common, shared context. This clearly relates to the IfL's belief in 'professional dialogue' and teachers researching into their own practice as the bases of meaningful CPD. Wells (1986: 221) refers to teachers as 'theory-builders' and states his belief that:

> Every teacher needs to become his or her own 'theory-builder' but a builder of theory that grows out of practice and has as its aim to improve the quality of practice. For too long, 'experts' from outside the classroom have told teachers what to think and do. They have even designed programs that are 'teacher-proof' in an attempt to bypass teacher involvement in the same way that so many teachers have bypassed student involvement.

Wells's criticism of '"experts" from outside' may bring to mind official advice and guidance and examples of 'best practice' which are considered to be transferable to any place of learning regardless of context. For some time now teachers in the compulsory sector have become accustomed to documents, CDs and DVDs demonstrating good practice arriving at their schools. In FE the 'Gold Dust' resources are admirable examples of the kinds of materials that can be produced by groups of people working together and they are often usefully adapted by teachers in the sector. However, the physical versions of the 'Gold Dust' resources can often be seen on staffroom shelves in serried ranks and in pristine condition. The difficulty with such materials is that they seem to be produced in 'context-free' environments and, as such, may not easily translate to a particular teaching and learning environment.

The idea that learning materials, resources and methods can be successful in one place and must, therefore, be successful in another place is part of a wider culture of 'best practice'. This links to some of the central tenets of managerialism and the contention that all places of learning are more or less the same and that methods can be uniformly applied regardless of context. An A-level teacher in a college sixth form centre; a literacy tutor in a young offenders' institution and a work-based learning assessor in a training provider could, no doubt, have interesting and useful discussions about what they do and how they do it and might learn much from each other. It seems unlikely, however, that they could develop a range of materials that would meet the needs of all, or indeed any, of their learners. The notion of 'best practice' is frequently extended to areas other than teaching and learning – to management, administration, funding and record-keeping.

James and Biesta (2007) undertook a large-scale longitudinal research project, published as *Improving Learning Cultures in Further Education* in which they develop a cultural approach to understanding learning. They argue for the transformation of learning cultures in FE based on their conclusions that all places of learning are particular and located in their own contexts and, while there will be many similarities, they are all unique.

> The cultural approach also enables us to adopt a different and in our opinion more realistic way to understand and manage the improvement of teaching and learning. The essence of this approach is to work to enhance learning cultures, in ways that make successful learning more rather than less likely. Because of the relational complexity of learning, and of the differing positions and dispositions of learners, there is no approach that can ever guarantee universal learning success, however success is defined. Rather than looking for universal solutions that will work always, everywhere and for everyone, the cultural approach helps us to see that the improvement of learning cultures always asks for contextualised judgement rather than for general recipes.
>
> (James and Biesta 2007: 37)

Even if you don't read the whole book, James and Biesta's conclusions, particularly the suggested 'principles of procedure' for transforming learning cultures in FE, should be required reading for anyone interested in improving teaching and learning. These conclusions also provide a good contextual underpinning for considering your CPD in its widest sense.

Setting the right tone – appreciative inquiry

Without recourse to long lists of academic references, it seems fairly well established that learners don't learn very well if they are simply told to learn without any explanation of why they should. They will not learn if they are made to feel that they are deficient in some way or if we don't try to build self-esteem and develop a sense of 'agency', that is, some belief that they can take some control over their own lives and learning.

Strangely, when people become teachers or engage in any other kinds of paid work, these ideas frequently aren't applied.

A model based on the 'delivery' of educational 'products', audited and inspected by external bodies can result in a blame culture which focuses on 'broken' teachers who need to be fixed. Realistically, there will always be some who aren't very good at their jobs; who don't treat their learners with respect and don't provide a very good service. Coffield (2008: 22) says:

> Post-compulsory education is not a job creation scheme for incompetent staff, who should be firmly but sensitively removed. The much greater problem is unimaginative and uninspiring teaching; and I suggest that we talk of 'poor teaching' rather than of 'poor teachers' on the principle that we castigate the sin but cherish the sinner.

The second part of this quote reminds us that very few people are beyond redemption. Many teachers who are not currently operating at their best might be able to do so if given appropriate support and encouragement. So how can this be done?

One way is for senior and middle managers to try to set a different tone and an atmosphere more conducive to improvement than a 'blame culture'. The principles of 'appreciative inquiry' were initially developed by David Cooperrider (1990) in the context of organizational change. Organizational change often flounders because of over-emphasis on negatives and deep inquiry into what's wrong. It may be necessary in cases of serious organizational failure to find out what went wrong prior to rebuilding. But, I would suggest, organizational change should be built on positives and on recognizing the existing strengths of the organization and all of its members. People, in this case teachers, are unlikely to improve by government or management dictat or because more procedures and systems are imposed to monitor them and ensure compliance.

Appreciative Inquiry (AI) takes a different starting point by suggesting that organizations should not focus their inquiries on what doesn't work or identify gaps and inadequacies; rather they should look at what *does* work and what are the existing strengths and abilities of its members. These kinds of inquiries are collaborative and predicated on exploring possibilities. The basic process of AI was originally built on the 4 D's – Discover; Dream; Design; Destiny. These may be a little too 'sugary' for some tastes; we prefer the 4 I's model:

> *Initiate:* Introduce the principles of AI to the whole organization and explain its core message of improvement built on positives. Get the 'big picture' of the project in place and identify areas to work on and people to work on them.

> *Inquire:* Get people talking and finding out about each other and themselves. Find out about what kind of organization they want and what they can do to bring it about. Unstructured or semi-structured interviews and focus groups are particularly useful. Encourage creative thinking. Listen without prejudice or preconceptions.

> *Imagine:* Collate and share the key themes which emerge from the inquiries and develop ideas and possible, even provocative, solutions. Share and validate them with as many people as possible.

Innovate: Begin the process. Keep people involved in conversations about the change. Review and adapt change in light of discussion and evaluation.

The essence of AI is encapsulated in the words of the old Johnny Mercer song: 'accentuate the positive; eliminate the negative; latch on to the affirmative'.

Learning organizations – the way forward?

One of the key elements of appreciative inquiry is that organizations should be creative in their organizational change and explore new ideas. Peter Senge, one of the leading writers on organizational learning, makes a distinction between *adaptive* and *generative* learning: 'The impulse to learn, at its heart, is an impulse to be generative, to extend our capability. This is why leading corporations are focusing on *generative* learning which is about creating as well as *adaptive* learning, which is about coping' (Senge 1996: 289).

Generative learning is a key characteristic of a *learning organization*. A learning organization is one which actively incorporates structures and processes to encourage and enable continuous learning and improvement. Senge (1992) describes the five 'disciplines' of a learning organization. The following account is a very brief overview of his ideas; for a more detailed discussion of his ideas in an educational setting see Martin (1999; Chapter 4). The five disciplines are:

1 Personal mastery
2 Mental models
3 Shared vision
4 Team learning
5 Systems thinking

Personal mastery

Personal mastery means every member of the organization having a personal vision of, and a belief in, what they can do. It's rather like the idea of 'agency' which we try to encourage in our learners; that is, the belief that you can make a difference and that you can make things happen rather than just having things happen to you. Teachers often feel, sometimes justifiably, the 'system', the management or their colleagues are working against them. Personal mastery means still hanging on to your personal vision, regardless of real or imagined threats. An ethos of 'appreciative inquiry' (see above) might be more conducive to personal mastery.

Mental models

Mental models could be described as our 'working models'. They are our conceptions of how we do things or how things should be done. In a learning organization each individual should be attuned to change; this involves challenging, and changing, our mental models. As Martin, writing about universities as learning organizations (1999: 59) says:

> Mental models are the prejudices and assumptions which inform our everyday thinking and doing. They are the things which get in the way of us working positively together and learning from experiences. Our commitment to mental models means that we are often not tuned to learning, but to defensiveness and appearing rational in advocating our existing positions.

Martin acknowledges that changing our mental models makes us feel vulnerable and is 'challenging and courageous'. However, if learning organizations intend to continually learn and adapt, then so must each individual within it. This links to the next discipline – shared vision.

Shared vision

In essence, shared vision is informed, possibly formed, by the sum of the personal visions within an organization. It is very similar to the 'inquire' and 'imagine' stages of the appreciative inquiry model. It is important that shared vision is a *commitment* based on the involvement of all staff, rather than *compliance* with an imposed 'vision'.

Team learning

In most educational settings we work in teams – subject teams; task teams; management teams. When they work well teams are extremely effective at producing things which are greater than any one individual could achieve. At their worst they can be counterproductive, competitive and emotionally damaging. In a learning organization teams collaborate to extend the pool of knowledge and to provide an arena for challenging personal and collective mental models.

Systems thinking

Systems thinking means that an organization and its constituent members can see the 'big picture' of the organization. It's about understanding how the parts contribute to the whole. 'Silo mentality' is a frequent metaphor used to describe people who work within a contained mental, and possibly physical space, without reference to the wider organization. The metaphor also has a defensive connotation in that those within it seek to repel outside influences with 'alien' ideas. Part of the managers' work is to help people have a holistic view of the organization and to see the benefits of cooperation and collaboration.

The principles and processes of structured CPD; appreciative inquiry and organizational learning can have a powerful effect on the development of meaningful and effective CPD in the lifelong learning sector.

Further reading and sources of information

The LLS operates in an environment of frequent policy shifts and refocusing of priorities and objectives. Teachers need to have an overview of the sector and be able to keep up to date with the most recent developments. The IfL guidelines for CPD recommend that teachers review the local and national contexts in which they operate. For example, those involved with Skills for Life will need to know the background to the introduction of Functional Skills and how they will impact on themselves and their learners.

The readings and sources suggested below provide some starting points for getting the big picture.

Further reading

Hyland, T. and Merrill, B. (2003) *The Changing Face of Further Education*. London: Routledge Falmer.

IfL (The Institute for Learning) This is the professional body for all those working in the LLS. You will need to download a copy of the IfL CPD Guidelines as a companion to this book. www.ifl.ac.uk

Intelligence e-Group For free regular email updates on policy, research and development news about the sector, join the Intelligence e-Group, by sending an email requesting that to mike.cooper@education-development.co.uk

LLUK (Lifelong Learning UK) is the sector skills council for the lifelong learning sector. All teachers should download a copy of the Professional Standards. Their publication *Lifelong Learning UK's Work for the Further Education Sector in England* is a useful contextual document. The site has numerous links to other relevant organizations and services. www.lluk.org

LSIS (The Learning and Skills Improvement Service) Provides a wide range of support, services and resources. The LSIS *Guide to LSIS Services* is a prospectus of all the services and is available in PDF format. www.lsis.org.uk

Ofsted Good Practice Database 'The Learning and Skills Sector Taxonomy' is a very good visual overview of all the relevant issues and elements related to the LLS. Available online at http://excellence.qia.org.uk/gpd

The Education Guardian The Guardian has an Education section every Tuesday. Available online at http://www.guardian.co.uk/education

The Times Educational Support This weekly publication is the main journal for those working in education. Its *FE Focus* section will be of most interest to teachers in the LLS, but don't ignore the main section. Available online at www.tes.co.uk

www.policywatch@edexcel.com Subscribe to this for regular policy updates.

2 Being a professional in the lifelong learning sector

> This chapter is about:
>
> - What is professionalism?
> - CPD as a professional responsibility
> - The role of the IfL in the lifelong learning sector
> - Professional rights and responsibilities
> - The IfL Code of Professional Practice

We find ourselves these days in uncharted waters, working in a newly defined sector, with relatively new requirements and regulations and also being asked to account for our own development to a new body – the IfL – that we are just getting to know. It is perhaps not surprising that teachers in the LLS often feel overwhelmed in terms of what they should be doing, why, when and for whom. This chapter aims to make this territory a little easier to navigate by providing a 'map' to show how our sector is now structured, introducing the bodies who now support us and watch over us and clarifying our own professional role within the sector in relation to CPD. Chapter 4 will provide more specific information about the variety of CPD activities and how to record them.

What is the LLS?

In order to fully understand this newly defined sector and our role within it, it will be useful to reflect on where it has come from and who it now includes before we consider what it means to be a professional within it. In essence, the LLS includes the further education sector, but along with a new name comes a new, broader remit. It now encompasses not only those involved in traditional further education but also those teaching in prisons, private training providers, local authorities, museums, archive facilities, libraries, community based education and the voluntary sector. The landscape now is significantly different with FE colleges offering learning to students as young as 14 and working in collaboration with schools to deliver the new Diplomas. As a result of various government reports (Foster 2005; Leitch 2006; DfEE 1999), learning is increasingly expected to take place in the work environment with the government providing some financial incentive for companies to offer their staff work-based, professional qualifications as well as literacy and numeracy in a bid to up-skill the workforce. Meaningful and measurable education within prison is also now high on the political agenda along with the 'hot potato' of access to higher education.

What is the IfL?

This significant shift in the sector meant that there was a requirement for an overarching body to provide professional standards and give a voice to professionals working in the new sector. This body is the Institute for Learning (IfL) which represents: teachers, trainers and assessors across further education (FE) including adult and community learning, emergency and public services, FE colleges, the armed services, the voluntary sector and work-based learning (www.ifl.ac.uk). The IfL use the terms 'teachers' and 'trainers' to include lecturers, teachers, trainers, assessors, instructors, tutors and trainee teachers. It would be too much of a mouthful to use all of the relevant terms when discussing job roles so please feel free to insert your own pertinent job title in place of teacher or trainer if that is more appropriate.

So, we know that the IfL exists to support this new sector, but how did it evolve? Discussions about having sector representation have in fact been going on since the late 1980s. In 1996, the Further Education Staff Development Forum (FESDF) was created, with one of their main priorities being to push for the introduction of national teaching standards in the FE sector. These standards were evident in schools but not in post compulsory education. Those working in FE were often seen as the 'poor relation' of the education sector, as staff were not required to hold a formal teaching qualification and many did not have subject specialist qualifications above level 3. The primary and secondary education sectors were very much seen as 'graduate professions' and terms and conditions of employment, particularly pay, were perceived to be higher than that in the FE sector. 1999 saw the FESDF converted into the Further Education Training Organisation (FENTO), with one of their strategic aims being to lobby for the role of a body to help with much needed 're-professionalization' of the sector. The Department for Education and Skills (DfES) approved FENTO's proposition for this professional body in 2001 and the first incarnation of the Institute for Learning (FE) came into existence. In September of that year, an ambitious target was set to have a fully qualified workforce by 2010. For the first time, the DfES and FENTO made it a requirement for those teaching in the newly defined LLS to hold a recognized teaching qualification. By 2004, a new name for the institution had been chosen to reflect its wider remit: the Institute for Learning (Post Compulsory Education & Training). The IfL's status as an independent professional body was confirmed on 2 January 2002. Importantly, between 2002 and 2006 a reform agenda was becoming evident in the sector, with various government reports and interested bodies, such as Lifelong Learning UK, scrutinizing the role and function of the FE teacher and investigating the need for a registered workforce. The IfL were influential in developing the regulations that were eventually adopted and from midnight on 31 August 2007, the Institute was ready to start accepting members. By the end of January 2009, there were more than 180,000 members.

Activity

- What do you think are the advantages of having a nationally recognized body representing the lifelong learning sector?
- Can you think of any disadvantages?
- What other professions do you know of that have nationally recognized bodies such as the IfL?
- Have a look at the IfL website at www.ifl.ac.uk and familiarize yourself with:
  - IfL's vision and strategy
  - membership benefits
  - latest news relevant to your sector.

The role of the IfL

The IfL has set out three strategic aims: *benefits*, *status* and *voice*. For the purpose of this chapter, we will focus on the aim of *status*. Under this heading, they have further identified four tasks to be addressed:

1 promote and raise the standard of FE and skills teachers and trainers and the profession as a career of choice
2 consolidate and build recognition of the value of teachers and trainers for their learners and the well being of the nation, its citizens and the economy
3 uphold the standards of professional practice
4 promote the licence to practice, through QTLS or ATLS [Associate Teacher Learning and Skills] as a marriage of subject expertise with teaching skills, knowledge and experience, complemented by a commitment to lifelong professional development

(www.ifl.ac.uk)

For the purpose of this chapter, we call these four tasks the four *aspirations* of status. In order to promote and raise the standards of professionals working in the sector, a new suite of teacher training qualifications has been in place since September 2007. There are now minimum levels of qualifications that staff are expected to achieve in order to demonstrate their competence and professionalism. All teachers in the LLS are now required to achieve their 'threshold licence to practice'. This is a stated level of competence and involves achieving an award called Preparing to Teach in the Lifelong Learning Sector (PTLLS). This qualification must be achieved within the first six months of starting to teach. This represents a significant shift in attitude. Since 2004, there has been a stipulation that teachers in FE should obtain a minimum level 4 teaching award within two years of being in post, however, there was little effective regulation or consequence if staff did not obtain the qualification. Crucially, there was no formal register of qualified teachers in FE and it was up to individual organizations to keep their own records. It was also arguably a 'one size fits all' approach, with the majority of staff having to complete a 2 year qualification regardless of their teaching role. Prior to 2004, there was no specific requirement for teachers in the sector to undertake teacher training. Can you imagine another profession where a minimum level of qualification was not deemed necessary or worthwhile? It was largely down to individual organizations to decide what qualifications it wanted its staff to hold along with its attitude to staff development. Under the new regime, there is a requirement that teachers start on their journey to become qualified right from the outset, with no exceptions. Along with obtaining PTLLS, teachers are now required to register with the IfL within 6 months of starting their teaching job. One of the many reasons for this is to try and introduce professional parity with teachers in the compulsory sector. So, if parity is the objective, does it not beg the question, why do LLS teachers not have to obtain a teaching qualification *before* entering the classroom? One strong argument against this is the vocational nature of the sector. We rely on experienced people coming into the classroom from their different professions and as such, demanding those people to give up their profession to embark on a full-time pre-service teaching qualification would inevitably reduce the pool of vocationally qualified, experienced staff available to teach. The sector is made up of many part-time teaching staff who still run their own businesses or continue to work in their specialist field and it is important that this status quo is retained. Classroom and workshops would be poorer places if teachers were not able to remain engaged in working in their vocational area. Of course, there are also many full-time members of staff who do give up their jobs to enter teaching or choose to complete their teaching qualification on a full-time basis but leaving that option open is vital for the success of the LLS.

So what happens once someone has achieved PTLLS? As this qualification is a 'threshold licence to practice', it denotes that someone is starting on their route to full qualification. Unlike the regime of the past when almost all teachers were expected to complete their Cert Ed or PGCE, the new structure gives teachers an exit point dependent on their job role. This again reflects the diverse nature of the sector where not everyone has what is now defined as a 'full teacher' role and highlights the differences between our sector and the compulsory sector. Some teachers, trainers or tutors have what is called an 'associate teacher' role. This acknowledges that they have fewer responsibilities in terms of their role although are still expected to demonstrate high quality teaching. If someone is defined as an 'associate teacher' then they will be expected to achieve the status ATLS by completing the CTLLS. If someone is defined as a 'full teacher' then they should be aiming towards QTLS by completing their full DTLLS. A brief overview of the difference in roles can be found in Table 2.1. This is just a quick checklist that might help determine a person's job role but full definitions and further details about the two roles can be found in the document 'Guidance for awarding institutions on teacher roles and initial teacher training qualifications' available on the LLUK website at www.lluk.org. It is also important to note that the requirement to complete one of the two qualifications is only for people working on publicly funded courses. There is no requirement for people teaching or training in the private sector to currently hold these qualifications.

Table 2.1   Overview of differences between the associate and full teacher roles

An associate teacher. . .	A full teacher . . .
Works mainly on a one to one basis with students	Teaches larger groups of students together in a class (groups could be defined as five or more students)
Teaches generally on one level of programme (i.e. staff on a training course or only learners on a short taster programme)	Teaches across a range of programmes (for example on level 1, level 2 programmes along with a module on an HNC)
Teaches similar types/levels of students (i.e. staff on a health and safety course or students on an enrichment activity)	Teaches a range of different abilities/levels of students (i.e. has exposure to working with different ability groups on different level courses)
Teaches on short courses (short programmes that may be one off or repeated short coursed)	Teaches on longer programmes

Of course, determining someone's job role may not be quite so straightforward, particularly when we have acknowledged how diverse the sector actually is; however, it is important to ensure that an individual is identified as falling predominantly into one of the two job roles to ensure that they are signposted onto the correct programme, either CTLLS or DTLLS. The programmes have not been designed to be completed in order; they have been designed to reflect a person's job role at any given point. This is then mirrored in terms of content in that relevant qualification. It may not therefore be appropriate for a person whose role sits quite firmly in the associate teacher camp to embark on the DTLLS programme as they will expected to discuss and evidence areas of practice that they are simply not involved in, nor have any need to be involved in.

It could be argued that the disadvantage of this new approach is that we determine a person's job role at a specific point in time. At that point in time, we might rightly define them as an associate teacher and point them towards the CTLLS route; however, six months later, their situation may change and they may find themselves in more of a 'full teacher' role, due to promotion or progression. It is often the case that teachers in the sector start out as sessional lecturers or assessors even though they may aspire to be full teachers, so defining them at one point in time does not take into account aspiration or progression. This point is particularly important if the LLS is to be a 'career of choice'. That said, the new regime does mean that a lot of people working in a specific job role in the sector are spared the time consuming process of completing a two-year programme when it is not appropriate and there is always the possibility of being able to carry on studying to complete the full diploma at a suitable time in the future.

What happens to those people who have been teaching prior to 2007? Do they need to complete a CTLLS or DTLLS programme in order to become qualified and be able to join the IfL? The answer to that is no. Any previous equivalent qualifications still stand, so someone who completed a Cert Ed or PGCE in 1996, for example, and is still teaching is not expected to do anything other than demonstrate their hours of

CPD. For those people who have no qualifications but were teaching prior to 2004, they may be able to get some accreditation of prior learning (APL) recognition towards the CTLLS or DTLLS programme but they will still be expected to become qualified.

Another development within this new structure is the notion of 'professional formation'. In the new arrangements just 'getting through' the qualification is not enough. Once the appropriate qualification has been achieved, the only way a teacher can actually be 'fully qualified' is by having this status conferred upon them by the IfL. This is done through something called 'professional formation'. This is described as:

> the post qualification process by which a teacher demonstrates through professional practice;

> 1 the ability to use effectively the skills and knowledge acquired while training to be a teacher
> 2 the capacity to meet the occupational standards required to be a teacher

> (www.ifl.ac.uk)

For those people employed after September 2007, there is a requirement that professional formation should be completed within five years of taking up a teaching position, be that as a full or associate teacher. For those qualified people who have been teaching before 2007, they are not required to go through the formation process, however, best practice suggests it would be a good way of demonstrating commitment and currency in their teaching practice.

Activity

- What previous teacher training qualifications do you currently hold?
- Are they appropriate for your job role?
- Have you been through professional formation?
- Are you a member of the IfL?
- What, if anything, should you do next in terms of your development?

Support for the IfL

The IfL has a significant role in terms of supporting staff, new and old, in the sector. It works alongside two other bodies: Lifelong Learning UK (LLUK) and Standards Verification UK (SVUK). These bodies have quite individual roles to play in supporting the IfL and teachers in the sector.

LLUK

This is the sector skills council (SSC) for the LLS, responsible for the development of teachers in the sector. In 2004, as a response to the report *Equipping our Teachers for the Future* (DfES 2004), LLUK was tasked with developing the new standards that would replace the FENTO standards, previously in place. They were set out in response to Ofsted's concern that new entrants to the profession needed to know exactly what was required of them. Equally, existing staff also required clear guidance as to what skills they should be demonstrating to ensure quality learning experiences for their learners. After consultation with interested and relevant stakeholders, in 2006, the 'New overarching professional standards for teachers, tutors and trainers in the lifelong learning sector' were introduced. Briefly, the standards are broken down into 6 domains (from A to F), with each domain being concerned with different aspects of teaching and learning, for example 'Professional values and practice' or 'Planning for learning'. These standards set out clear descriptors for staff to work to and provide the backbone of the new suite of teacher training qualification as mentioned above. There is more about the standards below in the section 'What is professionalism?'.

SVUK

This is a subsidiary of LLUK with a remit of verifying and endorsing the new teacher training qualifications. Organizations offering these new qualifications need to work with SVUK to demonstrate how their qualifications meet the standards. Standards Verification UK provides a tariff, which is a database of all other teaching and training qualifications that people might hold. The tariff is used to check how they map against the new suite of programmes at levels 3, 4, 5 and 6. Although this is actually only a guidance document, it is a good starting point for awarding institutions when thinking about APL processes and requirements. It can also be used to assess an individual's CPD needs, identifying any gaps that might need to be filled before going through professional formation.

The IfL's role in supporting and monitoring CPD

So, what happens once a trainee has finished their teacher training programme? There has finally been recognition that obtaining a teacher training qualification is only the start of the journey. We are now rightly expected to continue our development, post qualification. This is standard in many other professions, including in other phases of the education sector. This means that we now need to record our CPD and register it with the IfL on an annual basis. There will be more about the sorts of activities that constitute CPD in the subsequent chapters.

    If we go right back to the four aspirations of status outlined by the IfL, we can really start to appreciate the benefits of having a body such as the IfL. By ensuring that we have a strong qualification and post qualification structure, it should follow that there will be a rise in the standard of teachers in the profession; that they will be held in higher regard and will be valued as improving the well-being of the nation, its citizens and the economy. This can only be achieved by 'upholding the standards of professional practice' throughout our careers (IfL 2009a). It is vital that we, and the organizations we work in, make that commitment to improving our teaching skills and knowledge over the duration of our professional lives.

Continuing professional development is defined in the IfL's five year strategy document as the 'critical reflection on learning experiences and activities that improve practice and demonstrate continuous development as a teacher or trainer'. This supports the IfL's vision of having a highly performing, self-regulating work force that is committed to self-improvement. In the IfL *Guidelines for Your Continuous Professional Development* document (2009a), there is a suggestion that we break CPD down into 3 strands:

- updating teaching and learning
- updating subject specialism
- updating on national initiatives and the wider context.

This wider view helps us move away from merely walking out of a teaching session and thinking 'well, that was ok' or 'that didn't go as well as expected'. As professionals we need to ensure we are reflecting, reviewing and evaluating on a far wider level. Think of all the things that happen in education outside of the classroom, in other organizations, at local government level, at national government level. All these things impact on us and our ability to do out job effectively. This wider view will also help us meet the issues addressed in point four of the aspirations of status about improving our subject expertise or as it states 'the marriage' of teaching skills and subject skills. Teaching is not just about our skill in planning and facilitating learning; we also have to ensure we are working with the correct, most up to date, vocationally relevant information to our students. Organizations are now more aware of CPD and many put on CPD days or weeks during the academic year to help teachers meet their requirements. How much of that is subject specific? How is subject specific CPD monitored by your organization? How do you demonstrate this?

Activity

- Write a list of the last five CPD activities that you did
- Which of the three headings did they come under:
  - updating teaching and learning
  - updating subject specialism
  - updating on national initiatives and the wider context?
- Do you think you could evidence CPD effectively under all of those headings?

CPD – who benefits?

The simple answer should, of course, be everyone. As professionals, our CPD obligations are to our organization, our colleagues and the IfL. Above all, purposeful CPD primarily benefits teachers and learners. Those who have been working in the lifelong learning sector for many years may, in many cases understandably, have a jaundiced view of CPD and tend to associate it with end of year events at which all staff, frequently including non-teaching staff, were required to attend. These kinds of 'sheep-dip' activities were perceived by some of the recipients as being more to do with 'box ticking' within an audit culture. While it is true that many such events involved skilled and experienced teacher educators who provided valuable sessions, it is unlikely that any one event would be of equal value and relevance to all those attending.

Villeneuve-Smith et al. (2009: 13) write of the 'move from compliance to opportunity' and argue that the professionalization of the workforce 'changes everything – and arguably for the better'. Along with the notion of professionalization goes 'personalization'. Personalization has been, in recent years, a widely discussed concept – although much of the discussion has been about what personalization actually means. The personalization agenda has largely revolved around its use and development with learners; there has been little discussion of personalization in relation to teachers' personal and professional development. A key theme of this book is that teachers are learners; CPD is about learning. As Steward (2009: 1) states:

> personalisation of the professional development agenda recognises an individual's professional needs and engages them in activities that are important and relevant to them. Personalisation of continuing personal and professional development arises from an individual's professional needs and is a way of enabling staff to engage in lifelong learning themselves . . .

Professional subject specialist teachers are best placed to know what development and learning is necessary for them and their learners. Organizational systems should provide frameworks and support in which this personalized CPD can take place but which is driven by needs of teachers and learners. The new professional standards for teachers and the IfL CPD requirements give teachers a real chance to move from compliance to opportunity and to take the CPD initiative themselves. Many commentators have spoken of the decline in professionalism; the new arrangements may help to restore a feeling of autonomy in the lifelong learning workforce.

Professionals should be able to make professional decisions about their work. Effective CPD in the long term frees up time for better planning, time for innovation and even time to complete the necessary paperwork and it will also ultimately reward us with a better relationship with our students and may even have a positive impact on behaviour in our classrooms. We are going to get a better reception from our students when it is clear that we make an effort to plan and deliver interesting, enjoyable and relevant sessions, using the best resources available to us. Our passion and enthusiasm for teaching should be infectious, and students are likely to appreciate us more and work harder if they feel they are getting the best possible experience from us. We all enjoy the feeling we get when we have spent time and effort planning a session using a new piece of technology or a new teaching strategy and the session works wonderfully, with the students thanking us at the end for a great class. It's not egotistical to think like that, it is about providing the best student experience that we can. That's what real CPD is for.

Working in the lifelong learning sector is very demanding of our time and our emotional resources and, consequently, exhortations to undertake CPD, especially if it doesn't seem relevant, are not always welcome. However, we all need the impetus to challenge and re-motivate ourselves – CPD can provide this. You have probably been taught by or had colleagues who do not engage in CPD, often claiming they are too busy or that, even if they do it, they get no reward or recognition from management and, further, the students don't appreciate it. Even if at times we don't feel we are treated as professionals, it is incumbent on us to be professional. Moreover, in addition to simply fulfilling our professional obligations, well-planned CPD initiated by the teacher and supported by management can reinvigorate jaded careers.

Code of Professional Practice

As members of the IfL we agree to abide by its policies and procedures. We are expected to demonstrate that we are self-regulating professionals who understand and uphold the mission and values of the Institute, together with appropriate conduct and professional behaviour. One of the defining characteristics of a profession is that its members can be excluded if their behaviour is inappropriate or unprofessional and, in common with other professions, the IfL provides a code of conduct as part of the mechanisms to regulate professional behaviour. As members of a professional body, we must be aware of the kinds of conduct considered to be appropriate, necessary and expected. Details of these are set out in the Code of Professional Practice (www.ifl.ac.uk). As with any other professional body, there are consequences for not meeting these requirements. The IfL Code of Professional Practice 'defines the professional behaviour which, in the public interest, the Institute expects of its members throughout their membership and professional career' (2009d: 3). The Code of Professional Practice deals with issues such as professional integrity, reasonable care, criminal offence disclosure, respect and responsibility, and we are all bound by it as a condition of our continuing membership of the Institute. This is in line with standard practice in most other professions. We have to ensure that we meet the requirements of the Institute and behave in ways which are appropriate to a profession.

Disciplinary policy

The Code of Professional Practice sets out the procedures in case of concerns and complaints about members of the profession. In addition, it embodies a disciplinary policy and procedures. This is not necessarily a big stick to beat 'naughty' members with but a structure to ensure that people do not bring the profession into disrepute – again, this can be related back to the four aspirations of status that the IfL set out as one of their strategic aims. The Institute has to have credibility and appropriate powers to be able to promote and regulate professional standards and values.

The disciplinary policy is instigated only when it is deemed that a member has breeched the code of professional practice or if a member has been 'convicted of or cautioned for a relevant criminal offence'. In the first instance, an investigating officer will determine whether there are grounds to refer the case to an investigating committee. If this is found to be necessary, at the end of the investigating period, the committee will decide on one of three options which may involve the case being referred to the Professional Practice Committee. In the event of this happening, once the hearing is complete, a variety of sanctions are available including a reprimand, a conditional registration order, a suspension order or, in the case of a serious breach, expulsion from the Institute which effectively means being unable to teach in the sector. Further information about the disciplinary policy can be found on the IfL website at www.ifl.ac.uk.

What is professionalism?

> ### Activity
>
> - What is a 'profession'?
> - What does it mean to be a 'professional'?
> - Are you a professional? What is it about you that makes you a professional (e.g. education; experience; behaviour; values)?

Professionalism is difficult to define. If asked, most of us would like to define ourselves and our colleagues as professionals but what does this actually mean? When considering the concept of professionalism, we can take the discussion in many different directions but for the purpose of this chapter we will concentrate on the following aspects:

- three themes of professionalism – knowledge, autonomy and responsibility;
- a view of professionalism including rights and responsibilities;
- professional identity.

Lea et al. (2003: 60) state that 'textbook definitions of professional usually include a combination of the following characteristics: long training programmes in specialist knowledge; an ethic of altruism; autonomous work practices and the presence of a professional body'. Furlong (1998) echoes this, arguing that traditionally, the foundations of professionalism have been based on the three themes of *information, autonomy* and *responsibility*. The information theme suggests that becoming a 'professional' involves extended periods of study, for example studying for a degree or higher qualification. This education culminates in that person gaining substantial specialist knowledge and understanding. Typical examples of this would be the study and subsequent training undertaken by doctors, accountants, lawyers and, to an extent, teachers. Teachers' professionalism relies on them knowing and applying the theories that they have studied. This definition assumes that people who have not completed this level of study could never gain or demonstrate the necessary knowledge to call themselves professionals. Once this knowledge has been gained, professionals are granted autonomy by the government, and more widely, society, to practise their professions. They are trusted to practise in the way that they were trained and qualified to. If someone is needed to operate on a patient for example, clearly a doctor is the professional who is called and the doctor would expect to treat their patient appropriately, autonomously and without question. Following on from the notion of autonomy is the third theme of responsibility. A doctor demonstrates responsibility by acting within a set of appropriate professional values, based on professional judgement. Importantly, they always act impartially and independently, not on behalf of a third party such as a government. Furlong (1998) now argues that in the FE and LLS arena, these three themes that once defined a professional are now being gradually eroded by bureaucracy, reduced funding and an agenda of targets, control and accountability. This comes hand in hand with a challenge to the traditional notion of knowledge and, particularly from a postmodern perspective, that there is no certain objective knowledge. If this is indeed the case, then what value is there of a professional studying objective knowledge to a high level? Furlong reports a 'dissatisfaction with the notion that technical rationalist forms of knowledge (and most particularly the four "ologies" of education; sociology; psychology; philosophy; history) can guide professional action'.

So where does that leave us? If we accept the above as the defining characteristics of professionalism, can we apply them effectively to the LLS and the teachers that operate within it? How relevant is the notion of 'extended study' today? Does a two year part time diploma course equate to a period of extended study? Gleeson and James (2007) offer an alternative to the traditional notion of professionalism, suggesting that specifically in FE, people are becoming 'learning professionals', that is, someone who works in both an academic and vocational world where the environment is more complex but where the period of extended study is substituted for more practical 'on the job' experience.

Activity

Randle and Brady (1997: 131) suggest that professionalism in education includes the following:

- the primary importance of student learning and the teaching process
- maintaining loyalty to students and colleagues
- expressing concern for academic standards
- recognition of teachers as experts
- resources for education being made available on the basis of educational need
- some elements of autonomy being essential

- quality being assessed on the basis of inputs and processes
- maintaining a spirit of collegiality.

To what extent do you agree with these characteristics? Do they reflect your own perceptions of yourself as a professional?

Professional – rights and responsibilities

The notion of rights having concomitant responsibility has become a key theme in social and political ideas. We have become, according to some commentators, a society which expects to have rights but is less keen to accept the responsibilities that come with those rights; this applies to us as professionals in the LLS. It might be helpful to break this down a little further into an evaluation of our rights and responsibilities as teachers. Table 2.2 outlines some of the rights and responsibilities that could be associated with teaching in the LLS.

How do we demonstrate our rights and responsibilities and what happens if we don't? We frequently hear cases of professionals, not always teachers, who seem happy to expect and accept the privileges without considering the responsibilities that go with them. Formally acknowledging our rights and responsibilities is something that has been a recent development for the LLS. This view of professionalism for teachers in the secondary sector has been supported by the Teacher Development Agency (TDA) for many years and one of the reasons for setting up the IfL, as we have already discussed was to 're-professionalize the sector'.

We now have a comprehensive set of professional standards that help to define professionalism. The domains cover the following areas:

- Domain A: Professional values and practice
- Domain B: Learning and teaching

Table 2.2 Rights and responsibilities of professionals in the LLS

Rights	Responsibilities
Respect as a professional in our chosen field	Engagement with scholarly activity relating to either pedagogy or subject specialism
Autonomy to prepare, plan and deliver teaching sessions	Provision of relevant and timely CPD
Commensurate pay and conditions	Display appropriate conduct and behaviour towards students and colleagues
A voice at local and national level	
Status in the eyes of a community and wider society	Engagement with relevant industry and educational bodies including the IfL
Support from colleagues, managers and government	Commitment to an appropriate level of qualification

- Domain C: Specialist learning and teaching
- Domain D: Planning for learning
- Domain E: Assessment for learning
- Domain F: Access and progression

Each domain is broken down into three sections: professional values, professional knowledge and understanding, and professional practice. The professional values outline the underpinning ideals and principles that teachers should come into the profession with, ideals such as how learning benefits individuals 'emotionally, intellectually, socially and economically'. These values flow through all of the domains, whereas the individual standards under the headings of professional knowledge and skills and professional practice are domain specific. The standards are clear in their expectation and they set out our roles and responsibilities which in turn help to clarify our understanding of the level of professionalism we should be displaying in the sector. Where there may be some uncertainty is around the notion of professional identity and where it is in the standards. Studies have repeatedly shown that a person's view of professionalism is closely related to identity (Atkinson and Claxton 2000). The things that impact most on teachers' practice and their view of being professional are those things most closely associated with their own values and beliefs. Some of the issues of professional identity may be apparent in the dual professionalism debate. If you ask a plastering tutor what their profession is, do they say, 'I am a teacher of plastering' or 'a plasterer that does some teaching'? This perception of themselves may contribute to a conflicting view of their professionalism. It can be a struggle to encourage vocational tutors to engage with the professionalism required in teaching as they consider that their professionalism comes from their vocational practice, even though they may now be mainly engaged in teaching students. If teachers in the sector want the rewards of being involved in the teaching profession, we have to show credibility by engaging fully with the responsibilities that go with them. It is acknowledged however, that one of the issues regarding reluctance to gain a qualification is that of perceived academic ability. This lack of confidence can produce 101 different excuses from 'not having the time' to being 'too old'. With understanding and support, the vast majority of people do go on to prove that they are more than capable of completing the qualification and frequently give positive feedback about how useful and beneficial it has been. This is why bodies such as SVUK who verify the teacher training courses have a responsibility to ensure that the PTLLS, CTLLS and DTLLS qualifications provide people with the opportunity from both an academic and practical level to demonstrate their skills and understanding.

One particularly positive outcome of having the IfL is first, the requirement that people become qualified and second, having a body that takes an interest in this and monitors the sector to ensure it happens. If this engagement with qualification is not forthcoming, then the situation is clear – those teachers now have a choice to make: become qualified, demonstrate your professionalism or revert to working solely in the vocational field, away from students. Professional formation supports this view and employers are gradually becoming wiser to the fact that claiming government/public funding for courses means that qualified tutors are the only ones who can deliver this learning. It is absolutely right that teachers in the LLS should be appropriately qualified and should be looking to develop both the theoretical and practical side of teaching. As time goes on, with the help of the IfL the message of professionalism should continue to be promoted and expectations of working in the sector will start to change, with the result being that teaching in the LLS will have an appropriately qualified, credible workforce.

So what are the feelings of those working in the LLS? Gleeson and James (2007) explored what they called the 'paradox of professionalism' in a research project to examine the notion of professionalism in FE colleges in England. One of the reasons for the project was the identification of a new type of 'public sector professionalism' across sectors such as health, social care and welfare as well as education. It was acknowledged that with this new professionalization came increased levels of control, targets and accountability. Their paper reported the findings of the project that involved tutors in FE who worked as members of the research team and their view of how they 'constructed professional meaning' in their work. One particular area that was explored was how they became practitioners within the sector. Interestingly, the research confirmed the traditional assumption that teachers come into FE with little or no formal background or training in teaching. In fact, many expressed surprise that they had entered a 'professional' career, particularly as a teacher and several examples were given of situations when the teachers had 'slipped' into the role almost by accident. The report also outlined the idea of a 'long interview' where teachers did some part-time or sessional teaching before building up to a more full-time or permanent position. This is quite typical in FE and reiterates the need for the sector to be flexible in its recruitment practices. We have already agreed that the sector and individual teachers working within it can benefit significantly from maintaining roles external to teaching. In addition, the sector relies heavily on part-time teachers to remain flexible and able to respond quickly to changes. However, with this flexibility does come a possible disadvantage. Because of the uncertain nature of FE and the wider LLS, this flexibility can lead to the workforce being split into two distinct camps: the 'core' and 'peripheral' staff. This can make it difficult to build a coherent focussed professional team of staff, engaged in driving improvements forward. Another focus of the project was the idea that FE staff were often asked, driven by the organization's need to be flexible, to contribute to courses outside their areas of expertise. Several of the staff interviewed for the project reported that this had indeed happened to them. In addition, it was reported that in some cases, a sense of professionalism was diminished by a perceived movement from being a qualified subject specialist to a 'welfare worker' when teaching some of the younger students. This view is often backed up anecdotally within some of our teacher training sessions, particularly by staff teaching schools link or flexible partnership classes. Other stories to come from the project included the focus on external inspection, with its bias on teacher performance rather than student learning, and a sense that it is expected that you will act over and above your job role in order to support learners. When you consider these factors it is not surprising that we feel our sense of professionalism is challenged. More positively, the research found that the participating teachers did consider themselves to be professionals and recognized the responsibilities as well as the obligations that came with this. They were also able to 'exhibit subtle mediation skills' which allowed them to appear to be conforming with the rules and regulations but ensured that they provided meaningful learning experiences for their learners.

There are many aspects of professionalism that we haven't been able to touch on in this chapter but in essence, we have looked at different approaches to professionalism using the traditional definitions of information, autonomy and responsibility, however, acknowledging that we work in quite a specific arena where we can 'tinker' with some of those definitions. It is clear that the people teaching in the lifelong learning sector deserve to be classed as professionals. We are now engaging in study, mostly willingly, and could now be comfortably called 'learning professionals' where we acknowledge the hybrid role that teachers in the sector have. We do expect to have autonomy in our roles although again, autonomy is being questioned to a degree in most professions and is being replaced with targets, accountability and control. The vast majority of us continue to deliver our responsibilities on a day to day level with our students, peers and managers and we demonstrate what Wallace (2008: 68) calls 'a professional value base' striving to provide our students with the best learning experience possible. Teachers may sometimes feel that they are being asked to do more and more with less and less, but continue to believe in and value the benefits of education and get great rewards from seeing students succeed. We now have the benefits of being represented by a professional body, supported by clear professional standards. The sticking point for a lot of people is still the issue of qualification; however, the simple requirement of having to hold a qualification will ensure that over time the message will be reinforced. If we return to the four aspirations of status that the IfL set out, it is clear that even if all of them haven't been met at this time, we are well on the way to doing so.

Further reading

Crawley, J. (2005) *In at the Deep End: A Survival Guide for Teachers in Post Compulsory Education.* London: David Fulton Publishers.

Forde, C., McMahon, M. and Reeves, J. (2009) *Putting Together Professional Portfolios.* London: Sage Publications.

Robson, J. (2006) *Teacher Professionalism in Further and Higher Education.* London: Routledge.

Wallace, S. (2007) *Teaching, Tutoring and Training in the Lifelong Learning Sector.* Exeter: Learning Matters.

3 The reflective practitioner

Reflection is an important human activity in which people recapture their experience, think about it, mull it over and evaluate it. It is this working with experience that is important in learning.

(Boud et al. 1985: 19)

This chapter is about:

- The need to develop reflective practice
- Reflection, learning and development
- Barriers to reflection
- Mechanisms for supporting reflective practice
- Learning from lesson observations

Reflective practice is a fundamental element of improvement and the starting point of continuing professional development. Before you panic and think this is another tedious task for teachers to undertake, pause for one moment and consider your previous working and learning life. Are there things you would have done differently; decisions made in haste; particular turning points in your career which you could revisit and evaluate? While one cannot alter the past, reflecting on experiences and using the opportunities to develop and plan a way forward can be a positive way to initiate change, acting as a motivational tool to reinforce what you can achieve, not what you cannot achieve.

The need to develop reflective practice

Teaching is a profession and, in line with other professions, we have to maintain and improve standards by having a licence to practice. All teachers face the challenge of ongoing personal and professional development as well as responding to government initiatives, academic standards, technological changes, a diversity of learners and funding changes. What this means to the teacher, according to Burrows (1995: 347), is that 'If professional practice is about change, development and meaningful conscious action, the act of reflection becomes a pre-requisite'. The IfL confirms this by recognizing reflective practice as being an essential component of CPD for individuals in the lifelong learning sector (IfL 2008). The action to implement more rigour in the use of CPD, including reflection, developed from the Standards Unit publication *Equipping our Teachers for the Future* (DfES 2004), which highlighted the need for changes and improvements in the sector that would enable all learners to be taught by qualified and skilled teachers. Fundamental to this is the need for teachers to be committed to CPD, not only for their own development, but also for their learners and the institutions in which they work and to the continual updating and improvement of subject knowledge and the theory and practice of learning.

This commitment to CPD requires a positive self-concept and a belief that it's never too late to learn and to improve. Older, more established, teachers in the sector may feel jaded and overawed, understandably, by the constant flow of new initiatives, new technology and changes in their subject-specialism. The consequent feelings of a lack of autonomy and enthusiasm can be very de-motivating. However, a reflective and positive attitude to personal development can help to renew teachers' beliefs that they can make a difference and to develop a notion of self-efficacy. Bandura (1986: 391) defines self-efficacy as 'people's judgements of their capabilities to organise and execute courses of actions to attain designated types of performance'. Developing a positive notion of self-efficacy begins with reflective practice and evaluation of capabilities together with a willingness to embrace change and improvement for yourself and your learners. Coincidentally, self-efficacy and personal responsibility are precisely the kinds of attitudes that we are seeking to instil in our learners.

The value of reflective practice

Reflective practice in the LLS is aimed at:

- creating an inspirational workforce in the teaching and learning environment, achieved by means, of self-development, which should impact significantly on the quality of the learning experience and the teacher's/ learners' motivation;
- developing autonomy and a sense of self-efficacy;
- developing teachers as lifelong learners and 'change agents';
- driving CPD in order to maintain the IfL licence to practice;
- exploring new territory and looking for ways to develop as teachers in order to maximize the potential of the learners;
- mapping a way forward for individuals in their career pathways, to sustain interest and enthusiasm while working in the sector.

Activity

- Did you ever have a 'bad teacher'?
- Is there any such thing as a 'bad teacher'?

Reflect on how you reached that judgement. Did you look back objectively or did you reinterpret the past and produce negative associations because you didn't like the teacher or they didn't motivate you? On reflection was it due to lethargy, boredom or the teacher being out of date in their subject knowledge? Alternatively were the sessions being delivered in the same manner, for example, efficient, but didactic; or do you have a mindset there is only one way people should teach and learn?

- What could this teacher have done differently? How could they have changed?

Remember, if you do not act as a change agent and use reflective practice to develop and extrinsically motivate your learners you may end up mirroring the bad teacher you identified. So what interpretation do you have of CPD?

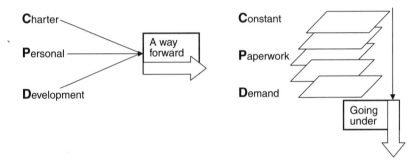

Figure 3.1   What does CPD mean to you?

The key word in the 'Charter for Personal Development' is 'personal'. If you regard CPD simply as a bureaucratic process that managers and the IfL require from you, then you will only undertake it grudgingly, if at all. If, on the other hand, you take a positive view of CPD as a means to make your professional work more effective and enjoyable and as part of being a lifelong learner, then CPD can be a liberating experience. Continuing professional development is, essentially, a learning process and, at this stage, it is appropriate to consider some relevant notions of learning.

Reflection, learning and development

In this section we will briefly review the development and application of some key theories of reflection, learning and development relevant to CPD.

John Dewey

John Dewey was a leading educational philosopher of the late nineteenth and early twentieth century. He believed that traditional education, as then practised in his native

America, was rigid, static and inappropriate for a rapidly developing society. Key to Dewey's philosophy was the development of thinking, particularly reflective thinking. In *How We Think* he asserts that, 'Thought affords the sole method of escape from purely impulsive or purely routine action' (Dewey 1933: 15). People who react impulsively are not in control. They are pulled along by events – things happen to them; they don't make things happen. To learn and develop we must move from routine action to reflective action, characterized by ongoing self-appraisal and development.

Dewey believed that reflection begins from a state of perplexity or doubt. Such situations may occur when you are a new teacher; when starting a new job; meeting new students; teaching something new. In such situations, two reactions are possible; first, ignore and don't adapt; second, use these periods of doubt and perplexity to learn.

Donald Schön

Schön's work (1983, 1987) is still influential in the development of reflective practice. Like Dewey, Schön believed that reflection and learning begin in uncertainty; in the 'swampy lowlands of practice'. The most relevant concepts from Schön, for our current purpose, are *reflection in action* and *reflection on action*.

> *Reflection in action:* This begins during your practice, in, for example, a teaching session. When something isn't working, one draws on past experience to reason why and to adjust the teaching and learning.

> *Reflection on action:* After the experience we can reflect on why the situation happened and consider how things can be improved. Solutions and changes can often be effected through discussion with colleagues or mentors.

> *Reflection for action* (O'Donnell et al. 2005): This concept develops from Schön's work and is concerned with using reflection as a basis for planning future action. There is little purpose in reflecting if no action results from it. Such action can form the basis for planning future teaching and learning and towards a cycle of continuous improvement.

A further development of Schön's work is the distinction between technical rationality and tacit knowledge. This distinction could be characterized as the 'theory–practice gap'. Teachers may have acquired the theoretical knowledge (technical rationality) of their subject and the associated pedagogy, but while this might explain their classroom practice as it should be, it might not explain it as it actually is. From these lived experiences teachers can develop tacit knowledge – a synthesis of theory and practice. This process may be developed further into action research (see Chapter 8).

Experiential learning

Experiential learning, often referred to simply as 'learning by doing', is according to Saddington (1992: 44): 'a learning process in which an experience is reflected upon and translated into concepts which in turn become guidelines for new experiences'. In essence it is about developing our professional practice from experiences and reflection.

The following models are examples of experiential learning. Such models are often referred to as *iterative*, repeating and based on cycles of activity.

Kolb

David Kolb (1976, 1984) devised a four-part cycle of learning based around the ideas of reflection and action. A simple version of Kolb's model could be:

- Do it
- Think about it
- Formulate a theory about it
- Do it again and see if it's any better

Honey and Mumford

Honey and Mumford (1992) developed Kolb's model further by suggesting particular categories, or types:

- Activists – prefer to launch themselves into activities, working on tasks from the outset;
- Reflectors – have a need to delve deeper into experiences through observation;
- Theorists – are logical and organized learners; learning is a construct of knowledge based on theory and reasoning;
- Pragmatists – have a preference for experimentation and action, the outcome of which might lead to intrinsic motivation.

No stage of this, or Kolb's, learning cycle is effective on its own. Individuals may prefer to launch into the preferred segment of the model from the outset. The main value of these models is that they encourage us to conceive of learning as a process of change and continual development.

Both Kolb and Honey and Mumford are included in the general category of 'learning styles' and, as such, require a word of warning. Much recent research (Coffield et al. 2004) makes serious criticisms of learning styles in general, suggesting that they are not based on any substantial or reliable research evidence.

Race's 'ripples on a pond'

Phil Race (2005) rejects the idea of cyclical models, preferring to use the analogy of 'ripples on a pond', in which the process ripples from the centre to the periphery and back, to understand learning. Working from the centre outwards, Race's categories of the learning process are:

- Wanting/needing
- Doing
- Digesting
- Feedback

Wanting and needing. The main difference between wanting to learn and needing to learn is where the motivation comes from. *Wanting* to learn suggests a personal, intrinsic motivation; something that the individual wants to do for its own sake, for enjoyment. *Needing* to learn might suggest an extrinsic motivation; something that is required by someone else or in order to undertake a new element in a job role. Needing to learn may not always be undertaken willingly. If the need and the want to learn coincide, then the individual is likely to feel more motivated.

Doing. This element of the model is about learning by doing; experimenting; 'having a go'. This can be an anxious, but, ultimately rewarding process. When the new teacher takes her first class or when the experienced teacher tries some new technology can be 'gateway' moments which affect their professional lives. The key to success at these times is the extent to which they are supported by colleagues and experts and how much risk-taking and experimentation are encouraged. The process of learning in this model could actually start with doing. If we take a new technology, for example blogging, we might not even see a use for initially, but familiarity with the technology can lead to application, even a want to learn it.

Digesting. This is about making sense of what we are learning. If we take a constructivist view of learning (see Chapter 6) this process is one of personal meaning-making. We can't just be given meanings by somebody else, we have to relate them to what we already know and our previous learning.

Feedback. This helps us to confirm our meaning-making. In discussion and collaboration with others we can check not only whether we have understood something but also we can develop it further and find new angles and applications.

Reflection, learning and development – other approaches

There are too many models and theories of reflection to discuss in this brief space, but the following may prove useful in your own reflection and development.

Transformative learning

The notion of transformative learning develops mainly from the work of Mezirow (1991) whereby a dilemma can lead to reflection and transformation not only of content but also of ourselves as teachers. It's about challenging our assumptions and presuppositions and changing our perspectives. This is reinforced by Moon (2004) who states that reflective practice is about having the capability and skills to facilitate the taking of a critical stance in relation to problem-solving and development. Reflective practice, in this formulation, involves moving out of our comfort zones and taking some possibly life-changing risks.

Critical incident analysis

This approach is associated with the work of Tripp (1993). Avis et al. (2010: 194) define and exemplify critical incidents:

A critical incident is that which we interpret as a challenge in the professional context. Tripp suggests that when something goes wrong, teachers need to ask what happened and why. It is therefore important that the incidents are framed as questions that the teacher asks him- or herself.

In this approach the reflection, and subsequent analysis, is based on a particular incident and the teacher starts to ask questions about what happened and why and seeks to find solutions which can be incorporated into their practice.

Collaborative learning

It is important to remember that reflective practice is not about negative criticism. Working with others in collaborative groups or 'learning circles' can be a mutually beneficial and rewarding approach. Working with peers can provide a safe place to try out new ideas and to take risks.

Critical lenses (Brookfield)

Brookfield (1995) suggests four perspectives, or 'lenses', through which we can examine and reflect upon our professional practice. The lenses are:

- *Our autobiographies as learners and teachers.* Our own experiences of being taught and our beliefs about what teaching and learning should be like will affect how we, ourselves, teach. Without reflection, there is a danger that we will teach in ways that we ourselves like to be taught.
- *Our students' eyes.* Brookfield (2005: 92) believes that: 'Of all the pedagogic tasks teachers face, getting inside students' heads is one of the trickiest. It is also one of the most crucial.' If we can try and empathize with our learners and try to imagine what it would be like if we were learners in our own classes, we can use this lens to reflect and adapt. There is a clear link here to the notion of emotional intelligence (Goleman 1995, 1998; Mortiboys 2005).
- *Our peers' perspective.* Allowing peers to observe our work and to discuss it with us can illuminate areas for improvement which we might otherwise be unaware of.
- *Theoretical perspectives.* It is important for us to return to and read theory because it provides a basis for understanding and improvement. We may be aware of something wrong and theoretical insights, while they may not provide an answer in themselves, can give us a starting point.

Appreciative inquiry

As discussed in the opening chapter, appreciative inquiry is an extremely important, possibly transformational, approach not only to reflective practice but also to personal and organizational change and development. For the purpose of our discussion of reflective practice the appreciative inquiry approach provides an antidote to an ethos of criticism and negativity about what people can do and suggests that learning and development is not primarily about looking for gaps or deficiencies in our knowledge and practice, but about actively searching for possibilities for change and new ideas and approaches. In politics and business this is sometimes referred to as 'blue sky thinking'. The work of Orem et al. (2007) is a good starting point, suggesting that appreciative inquiry, or appreciative coaching, is a collaborative approach to developing individuals based on a positive attitude in which honesty, trust and integrity are maintained throughout the process.

Figure 3.2 is a visual synopsis of reflective practice which combines the theoretical perspectives discussed above.

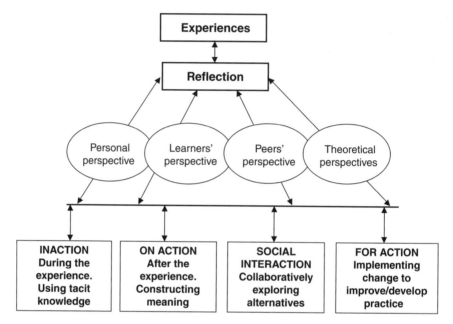

Figure 3.2 A composite model of reflection based on Schön (1983), Brookfield (1995) and O'Donnell et al. (2005)

Activity

- Having considered a range of theories and models of reflection, which, if any, will be useful to you in your practice?
- There are criticisms of reflective practice which suggest that it is too theoretical or self-absorbed. To what extent do you agree with such criticism? How can we use reflection practically, avoiding excessive 'navel gazing'?

These questions may help to clarify your own thinking about reflective practice and to consider potential barriers to reflection.

Potential barriers to reflection

While reflective practice is an important skill to develop, teachers and organizations need to be aware that there can be misconceptions about it and potential barriers to it, for example:

- *Stress:* it could be seen as time consuming, which could put some teachers under more stress;
- *Apprehension:* concern that identifying weaknesses or problems may have a detrimental effect in an organization;
- *Organizational ethos:* little or no support for reflective practice or recognition of its value;
- *Realistic/unrealistic:* identifying strengths, but no weaknesses;
- *Prejudice:* it's just another educational fashion which will pass;
- *Confidence:* concern that highlighting strengths may have an adverse reaction from others in the team;
- *Collaboration:* unwilling to share and develop experiences with others.

Now that you have an insight into the purpose of reflective practice and have considered some of the potential barriers, you can begin to reflect for action and adopt a positive attitude to developing your professional practice. Reflection can be a rewarding activity but it can have a strong emotional impact.

Reflection – an emotional challenge

An emotionally intelligent person is one who can recognize and manage their own emotions and those of others. For CPD this is important in terms of the way you handle your own emotions, particularly those resulting from reflection and responses from colleagues, and the emotions of your learners to help you understand their motivation and learning. The concept of emotional intelligence developed mainly from the work of Goleman (1995, 1998) who identified five 'social and emotional competencies' (Goleman 1998: 318). These are:

- Self-awareness: being alert to your feelings
- Self-regulation: managing your feelings
- Motivation: using feelings to help you achieve your goals
- Empathy: tuning in to how others feel
- Social skills: handling feelings well in interaction with others

Some individuals have more emotional intelligence than others, meaning they can deal with emotional challenges, whereas others find this more difficult. How you handle and manage your own and others' emotions can impact significantly on your attitude to and development of reflective practice; clearly, an 'appreciative inquiry' approach (see above) is preferable because it focuses on positives rather than negatives.

There is a clear relationship between reflective practice, emotional intelligence and professional development. As Mortiboys (2005: 132) points out:

> The use of structured reflection as a tool for learning is common in professional development and is inseparable from the process of developing emotional intelligence. Just as emotional intelligence is essential for effective reflection, so the reflective process is essential in the development of emotional intelligence. Reflection is about learning from experience. In order to learn from experience it is invariably necessary to take account of the emotional component of the experience . . .

Mortiboys (2005: 131–9) provides a range of very useful activities to support the development of emotional intelligence in professional development.

Activity

Consider an experience when either teaching or in a learning environment when there has been an emotional element, for example anger or hostility.

- How effectively did you handle the situation?
- What worked or did not work?
- Are you aware of any reflections following this that led to changes or improvements in how you work with learners?

While it may appear an emotional challenge to develop a meaningful insight into experiences, Claxton (2001: 146) recognizes we are sometimes in a quandary following experiences; however we should turn this around to view 'a new way of conceiving the problem'. A means by which we can do this is by using reflection and action planning.

Mechanisms for supporting reflective practice

The mechanisms used for evidencing reflective practice can vary, with a personal preference being the key to encouraging individuals to engage in a course of action. These include:

- Personal Development Journals (PDJs)
- Online discussion boards
- Portfolio of evidence of CPD
- Learner feedback
- Teaching and learning observations, including personal reflection and evaluation

- CPD periodic reviews with mentor
- IfL (summary of CPD), with the option for online reflection.

Personal Development Journals

One of the most frequently used methods of reflection is the PDJ in which individuals undertake an ongoing self-dialogue, including recording and reflecting on critical incidents. The use of a journal can be an excellent record of distance travelled and helps you to identify key themes in your development and signposts for the future. A PDJ also plays an important role in developing a critical approach to learning and personal development. Critical events should be recorded in your journal as soon as possible, and as accurately as possible, after the event while they are still fresh in your mind. Once recorded, the reflection, analysis and evaluation can be considered at greater length.

The manner in which Gibbs (1988) suggests we can carry out this reflective practice is summarized below:

- *Reflectivity* – What happened? Note what was observed from the experience.
- *Affective reflectivity* – identify your innate response to this situation. What are your feelings about the situation?
- *Discriminant reflectivity* – make notes of what you did and on what basis you took this action. Question whether it worked, and whether you have anything that confirms it worked, for example, questioning self-perceptions.
- *Judgemental reflectivity* – consider whether you have pre-judged events or made assumptions. Consider on what basis you made a judgement of an incident and where that judgement came from. Also, question whether you have ever asked for advice, or whether you always make your own judgement and stick with it.
- *Conceptual reflectivity* – think about your perceptions and values and the ways in which these might affect how you make sense of events.
- *Theoretical reflectivity* – consider how knowledge of specific theories is influencing your teaching/learning and ways in which you can assess their value.

Reflective practice doesn't come naturally but can be practised and developed over time. This has been reinforced by research undertaken with trainee and in-service teachers on our courses. The following is a summary of key issues raised by 100 students:

- The majority of students could define the word 'reflection' at the start of the course.
- At the early stages of developing a PDJ, the majority of individuals saw little or no purpose in using it.
- Initially it was just a descriptive account of what was happening.
- Difficulty of being analytical when new to teaching.

- If the PDJ is assessed, it can be tough to be honest. You might put what you think is required by others, not what you want to put.
- Not everyone likes writing a PDJ.
- The mentor can adversely affect the process of using reflective practice if they are not fully committed to the principle of reflection for action.

They also identified these strengths when using a PDJ:

- Looking back at keeping a journal, respondents in the research were encouraged by the distance they had travelled.
- Even though teaching may not be a new experience, a journal can be an excellent means for implementing changes, which can be seen to work.
- The journal can make you proud of your developments. If you are honest you can face up to the challenges of improving and work with others to develop.
- A PDJ is a very positive means for having an emotional outlet, including visuals that reinforced the positive events and the negative occurrences.
- PDJs enable you to get to grips with your CPD and take some responsibility for self-development.
- PDJs are an excellent way to link theory to practice. They were considered especially valuable to integrate PDJ extracts into coursework assignments.

What also emerged was that a PDJ should not be too prescriptive as this can be demotivating. Teachers and trainees should be encouraged to develop a format which suits their personal needs and style, for example:

- making written accounts of critical events;
- using visual images to highlight or reinforce events, for example positives or negatives;
- using diagrams to understand, analyse and evaluate events;
- leaving spaces to return to and add relevant theory notes or subsequent ideas;
- creating and developing an action plan, linked to the journal and teaching observations which establish a framework for ongoing development;
- including cuttings, quotes, drawings and a wide range of devices to record and interpret events.

The research evidence also suggested that reflective practice develops through stages, with increasingly insightful levels of thinking evolving over time. However, one model does not fit all and alternative methods for recording and interpreting critical events need to be available. Prescribed methods of journal writing without a clear understanding of purpose and value can result in routine, descriptive accounts lacking insightful understanding of events. Moon (2004: 134) refers to this as 'superficial reflection' which fails to yield deeper understanding.

Online discussion boards

Ganley (2004) emphasizes that teachers cannot initiate change with learners if they are not prepared to test out different strategies, using technology for example, and to reflect on their use in terms of thinking, research and creativity. The development of online discussion boards and blogs provides opportunities to broaden our horizons and explore different ways of developing professional practice using a more collaborative approach. The British Educational Communications and Technology Association (BECTA) discussion paper *British Educational Creativity to All* (2007) states the importance of building links between formal and informal learning. This can be undertaken using technology, to work collaboratively in order to reflect, share strengths and acknowledge and reflect on how weaknesses can be developed. These technologies allow us to develop wider communities of practice and develop a questioning approach to resolving problems related to teaching and learning.

Koschmann (1996) refers to computer supported collaborative learning (CSCL) environments and their role in supporting and developing collective thinking and professional development. Research in this area suggests that using technology to support collaborative learning is growing and becoming more sophisticated. However, McMurray and Dunlop (1999) argue that technology which supports wide networks of participants will not, of itself, produce collaboration. The key to success, they suggest, is not the technology but a shared conception of teaching and learning based on co-constructionist principles in which participants are motivated to build knowledge together.

> If meaningful and useful collaboration is to become an integral part of computer assisted education, it is essential that the students are motivated to participate. It is crucial, therefore, that there are shared goals with the purpose of collaboration having been agreed by all participants.
>
> (McMurray and Dunlop 1999: 6)

The conclusions from the research concerning the use of technology and collaborative learning are reflected in the outcomes of a small-scale research project with trainee teachers at the University of Derby (Headley 2009). What was apparent from this research was that computer supported collaborative learning does not suit all teachers, and, indeed, learners, and that different students will have different attitudes towards its use and value. However, the respondents in the research noted a number of positive aspects of this use of technology, including:

- a good support mechanism when feeling demotivated;
- an emotional outlet;
- a positive way to stimulate the brain and think through and try to understand experiences;
- a good opportunity for social networking including, importantly, having some fun;

- important for building skills and confidence by sharing experience with others;
- contact with others in the same subject specialism.

Lave and Wenger (1991: 37) believe that professional development is about 'working both independently and collaboratively to construct knowledge through inquiry-based learning'. There are advantages to working within networks in which learners are already known to each other and 'being supported by people with whom they can identify' (Beetham et al. 2007: 123), although there are difficulties with learning online whereby there is no personal identity. This was supported by our research which suggested that people who socialized together responded very positively to using reflective practice combined with social interaction.

It seems clear from the published research and the work with our students that while technology is vital in supporting a collaborative framework it is more important that teachers and students develop a shared conception of constructivist and co-constructivist principles of learning to support building knowledge together; put simply, a move from knowledge reproduction to knowledge creation.

Portfolio of evidence

The IfL has stated its intention to be rigorous in monitoring members' CPD and to maintain the professional standards of the Institute. While the IfL has not prescribed what evidence should be compiled in portfolios to illustrate CPD, there are recommendations for content as follows:

- reflective accounts which reaffirm strengths and highlight areas that could benefit from changes;
- the initial action plan and targets;
- evidence of CPD, for example:
  - qualifications
  - conference attendance
  - development of new resources
  - use of ICT
  - researching new developments in the sector.

Compiling a portfolio can build confidence and confirm the hard work and commitment individuals are making and, as such, can serve to motivate further learning and development. However, the main purpose of the portfolio is to demonstrate reflection and development; it is not an end in itself. As Scales (2008: 15) states 'It is not about the production of mountains of paper evidence at the behest of teacher trainers or managers'. Portfolios and PDJs are not just filing exercises.

Learning from lesson observations

Observation and evaluation of teaching and learning are key elements in improvement, both at an individual and institutional level. As a reflective practitioner you will develop the habit of 'observing yourself', in the sense of being aware of your activities and interactions in the classroom or workshop and making adjustments as you go along. Trainee teachers, in particular, need to reflect on and evaluate their sessions during and afterwards and identify good and emerging practice as well as considering what went less well and how it can be improved. It's a good idea to ask yourself a few general questions immediately the session has finished and follow this with more considered reflection later.

Some general questions to ask yourself immediately after the session

- What were you planning to do or wanting the learners to achieve?
  ○ Who are the learners?
  ○ How were you trying to achieve the session aims and objectives?
- What happened?
- What went well?
- What was effective? How? Why?
- What went according to plan? What didn't?
- What were the causes of difficulties/changes, etc?
- What would you do again?
- What wouldn't you do again?
- What was unaccounted for/not planned for?
- How will your planning for the future change?

It's a good idea to include some of your reflections in your journal and to link your thoughts and observations to learning and teaching theory. Busy teachers in the lifelong learning sector may find the idea of keeping a journal something of a chore but it can be an extremely useful aid to reflection. Keeping a journal is also an important element in action research projects (see Chapter 8).

Being observed

Observation of teaching and learning is part of the quality procedures in all learning institutions. Grading observations of teaching is a thorny issue and many teachers are wary about what the grades are used for, particularly at times when redundancies loom. Many colleges and providers give their teachers a numerical grade; others use particular words or phrases to describe performance such as, excellent; very good; good; satisfactory; inadequate. Whatever system is in place, the main purpose of observation should be improvement rather than grading. Undertaken in the right spirit, observation should be supportive and developmental.

The observation process should, ideally, involve:

- a time and date mutually agreed by observer and observee;
- ample notice allowing the observee to prepare;
- agreed and shared criteria and format for observation;
- developmental feedback provided as soon as possible after the observation;
- action planning for improvement following observation and feedback;
- support for improvements.

Observers should be skilled in, and preferably trained in, observation procedures, particularly how to give sensitive and developmental feedback. If the relationship between observer and observee is positive, it might be a good idea to negotiate a focus for your observation. You could, for example, agree a focus on your classroom communication and interaction, or your use of questions.

Peer observation

Peer observation is encouraged by many learning providers and can be a more supportive and less threatening activity than an observation by a manager or a member of an observation team. The process of observation is voluntary and involves two, or perhaps, three colleagues agreeing to observe each other. There are obvious advantages on both sides: the observee can get useful advice and suggestions from their observer colleagues; the observers can see different or novel approaches that they haven't previously been aware of.

Aims of peer observation

The main aims of peer observation and development are:

- To contribute to a culture of teamwork and mutual support
- To reinforce reflective practice that leads to improved learning for students
- To encourage innovation with support from peers: a developmental approach.

Objectives for peer observation

- To encourage CPD
- To stimulate improvements in teaching and learning
- To improve teachers', especially new teachers', confidence
- To foster discussion and dissemination of good practice
- To stimulate further research.

Some principles and ideas for peer observation

- It should be voluntary.
- It should be non-judgemental.
- It should be supported by management but run by and for teachers.

- Each pairing/triad could have a specific, agreed focus.
- Peer observation could be supported by reading and research, perhaps even an action research project.
- Peer observation and review could take place across partnerships with schools, employers and training providers, particularly in Diploma teaching.

Reviews and appraisals

Everybody working in the lifelong learning sector will be required to have appraisals of their performance, usually with managers, and set agreed targets for development which meet the needs of the teachers and the learners but are also in line with the organization's mission and objectives. New teachers may also have meetings with mentors to support them in their development and to review their progress. Without careful planning, preparation and a supportive framework, such meetings can seem to the participants little more than bureaucratic exercises; handled well, they should be valuable to the individual teacher and to the organization. The following are some examples of development targets and activities which could emerge from reviews and appraisals.

- upgrading subject-specific knowledge and skills;
- work placement visits;
- developing links with local employers;
- developing links as part of a Diploma partnership;
- further study for advanced qualifications;
- becoming an external verifier or external examiner;
- action research projects;
- writing articles for journals or websites. These might be based around action research carried out with colleagues;
- providing staff development sessions for colleagues in your subject specialism;
- visiting conferences or training sessions;
- 'cascading' information and ideas from attendance at conferences and training sessions;
- becoming part of or setting up learning communities, possibly in your subject area;
- becoming a Subject Learning Coach;
- some organizations have advanced practitioner posts for experienced and excellent teachers;
- developing new courses or curriculum areas in response to recognized need in the organization, local business or the community.

Mindset

Our beliefs about our own skills and abilities can affect our attitudes towards learning and development, positively or negatively. Carol Dweck of Stanford University has researched the area of self-belief over several decades and her findings have implications for own development as teachers and for our learners. Her most recent development of this research is expressed in the idea of 'mindset' (Dweck 2006).

Dweck suggests that people tend to have either a 'fixed mindset' or a 'growth mindset'. Those with a fixed mindset believe that their basic abilities, such as intelligence or talent, are fixed traits which cannot be changed. They also believe that talent alone creates success not effort or practice. A 'growth mindset', on the other hand, recognizes that brains and talent are just the starting point and that effort and purposeful engagement will result in improved performance and continually developing ability. The concept of fixed, ability particularly fixed intelligence, is still pervasive in societies such as ours and serves as a limiting factor for many children and adults. Robert Sternberg, currently one of the foremost researchers on intelligence, states that a major factor in achieving expertise 'is not some fixed, prior ability but purposeful engagement' (Sternberg 1997: 1031).

Teaching which helps to develop a growth mindset increases self-belief and, consequently, motivation. Many of our learners in the LLS will be coming to us with negative experiences of learning; encouraging a growth mindset can help them to break out of fixed beliefs about their ability. These ideas are echoed in Claxton's work on *Building Learning Power* (2002; see Chapter 6). Hart et al. (2004) write persuasively about the limits of education based on fixed ability and make a plea for a move from 'ability-based' to 'transformability-based' pedagogy. Part of the continuing professional development of teachers, especially in this sector, should be to research this pedagogy and to find ways to transform their teaching.

> We can now see more clearly how the transformability mindset frees teachers ... restoring their full power as educators, their power to use their knowledge, expertise and creativity to make a significant difference, and not just a small difference, to young people's future lives.
>
> (Hart et al. 2004: 246)

The QUAD model of development

We all have a need to experience positive feelings about our teaching and to feel that what we do makes a difference to our learners and to ourselves. There will be highs and lows in everyone's career and times when the job doesn't seem worthwhile and nothing can make any difference. Becoming a more reflective practitioner can help us to realize that we can be proactive rather than reactive and seek to question, understand and improve our practice. Figure 3.3 shows a process model to help you think about and relate some of the key principles and questions when using reflection for CPD. Some examples are given under each heading below.

Question   – critical events; positive and negative experiences
               – recurring themes
               – your experiences
               – your attitudes and opinions

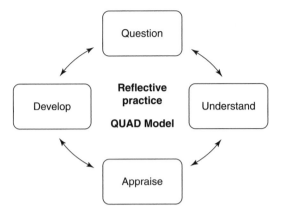

Figure 3.3 The QUAD Model for reflection and continuing professional development

Understand – links between theory and practice
– the value of collaborative working
– different perspectives
– learners' needs, for example, additional support; learning styles; cultural differences

Appraise – your PDJ; monitor your progress
– learners using formative assessment
– learners' attendance and achievement
– and evaluate feedback from learners

Develop – using teaching observations to identify themes for development and to set targets
– through reviewing PDJs and action plans
– using appraisals and periodic reviews
– by researching, applying and evaluating new teaching and learning techniques
– by using reflective practice and CPD to maintain your licence to practice

Reflection: the way forward

Reflective practice has become embedded in educational discourse and educational practice. This does not mean, however, that it is accepted and valued by those working in education – reflection and reflective practice are not without their critics. Reynolds and Suter (2010) offer a brief survey of the literature from which they provide a summary of four main areas of concern:

1   Doubts about the efficacy of the reflective process
2   To what extent organizational cultures are enabling of reflective practice

3 The fact that the wider context of teachers' practice may not be supportive
4 Scepticism about teachers' commitment to reflective practice.

On the final point Suter (2007) warns that reflective practice can become 'routinized' and just another chore which teachers are obliged to carry out but one in which they see little utility or value. For reflective practice to have a chance of success it must be valued for its own sake as a process of development and improvement and not, primarily, as a process which is undertaken, monitored and evaluated by others. We have probably all seen evidence of these concerns in our own organizations and anecdotally. One of the main purposes of this book is to enable teachers, managers and organizations to see the value of reflective practice and to make it part of the organizational culture. The IfL's new CPD philosophy is a real opportunity for teachers to take control of CPD and to locate it firmly in their own practice and understandings. If we want to 're-professionalize' teaching it is important that individual teachers take the lead and use reflective practice to begin the process of CPD. Perhaps the understanding and development of reflective practice is the first step in the CPD process.

Further reading and sources of information

Liverpool John Moores University. JMU Learning and Teaching Press *Approaches to Learning and Teaching Reflective Practice*. http://www.ljmu.ac.uk/lid/LID_docs/ISSUE_02_ReflectivePractice.pdf
This is intended for university but it's still an excellent introduction with some references to reflective practice in a range of subject disciplines.
Moon, J. (2004) *A Handbook of Reflective and Experiential Learning: Theory and Practice.* London: Routledge.
Includes some very useful photocopiable resources to support reflection and reflective writing
Moon, J. (2005) *Guide for Busy Academics No. 4: Learning Through Reflection.* York: Higher Education Academy.

Websites

Appreciative Inquiry
http://www.new-paradigm.co.uk/introduction_to_ai.htm

Learning and Teaching
Atherton, J.S. (2009) *Learning and Teaching: Reflection and Reflective Practice* [Online]. Available at http://www.learningandteaching.info/learning/reflecti.htm

Skills for Life Improvement Programme
Developing Reflective Practice in the context of Literacy, ESOL and Numeracy: http://sflip.excellencegateway.org.uk/workforcedevelopment/reflectivepractice.aspx

4 The CPD process

As outlined in the previous chapter, reflective practice is the starting point in helping you to identify your own continuous professional development needs. This is reiterated by the Institute for Learning (2009), which states that it is this 'critical reflection on learning experiences and activities' that actually drives forward the improvement of practice and your continuous development as a teacher or trainer.

This chapter is about:

- The CPD process – getting started and planning
- How CPD is informed by reflective practice
- CPD example case studies/activities/tasks
- How CPD may be recorded and monitored

As professionals we aim to create the best conditions possible for our learners to achieve. Hillier (2005) also argues that a main focus of professionalism includes striving for 'excellence'. We cannot strive for excellence if we do not know how well we are doing or how effective our learning programmes have been. The starting point for your own CPD, therefore, must be critical reflection on your own practice and action planning for improvement following evaluation and analysis of activities undertaken.

Getting started

You need to be able to identify your own professional development needs in order to prioritize and inform your CPD. A starting point is outlined by the IfL (2009a) which suggests you consider *two* parts relating to your professional identify, i.e. your subject specialism and your teaching. Teachers in the LLS are very often professionals in their own subject field before starting a teaching career. You may be working in, for example, the travel and tourism industry, sports or business sectors or engineering before changing your career and teaching your subject specialism. You then need to consider the teaching aspect of your professional 'role' as both parts of your practice are equally important. As well as keeping abreast of changes in your own subject specialism, you need to be actively involved in teaching and learning activities and new ideas emerging from best practice in your development as a practitioner. Taking responsibility for your own work and development is often referred to as self-regulation. Indeed, Robson (2006) suggests the three components of professionalism are: professional knowledge; autonomy; and responsibility. You have a responsibility to behave in an appropriate way and ensure fairness and impartiality. In the classroom environment you will have to deal with a variety of situations and it is your experience and expertise that will enable you to cope with the challenges you encounter.

It could be argued that some key benefits of the CPD process support not only your own professional development but also development on a personal basis, providing a clear structure for ongoing continuous and meaningful improvement. Your own development, therefore, through a recognized and planned CPD process will enable you to achieve your stated professional and personal goals. Hitching (2008: 2) believes that, 'a system that supports entitlement to CPD will also, over time, increase career choices and opportunities to promote greater autonomy for individual practitioners'. This reinforces the notion that the sector as a whole will benefit from a systematic approach to CPD, as teachers, lecturers and trainers enhance career development and take responsibility for their own professional development on an ongoing basis throughout their careers.

Reflective practice

You will need to reflect on any external factors, such as government legislation and policy initiatives and internal factors, such as curriculum priorities, budgets and staffing, that may affect your focus for CPD activities as 'both parts of your professional practice are equally important' (IfL 2009a). The actual context in which you work (college; training provider; your subject specialism) and your organization's priorities will also impact on your CPD planning. Priorities change and plans can be amended to accommodate them as particular elements of the various considerations may take priority over other aspects. You must be adaptable, flexible and forward thinking in your approach to CPD as the LLS is continuously developing.

Dual professionalism and the impact on your CPD

As can be seen from Figure 4.1 (IfL 2009a), the drivers of CPD have been categorized into three main elements to take account of your subject specialism, your teaching and learning (*dual professionalism*) and your organization's priorities, which will be influenced by indicators such as external inspection, self-assessment and policy initiatives.

We can consider an example of how these three elements of CPD interact by taking the example of Skills for Life. Skills for Life developed from the Moser Report *A Fresh Start* (DfEE 1999) which identified the numbers of people who had literacy and numeracy problems. The government's response was to introduce the Skills for Life strategy (2001) and, clearly, this placed an obligation on learning providers and their staff to meet the needs of learners within the Skills for Life strategy. Teachers needed to be skilled and trained to deliver literacy and numeracy, and later ICT, in ways that were relevant and meaningful to learners, preferably embedded in vocational or subject contexts. The introduction of Functional Skills will have similar impacts on context, subject specialism and teaching and learning.

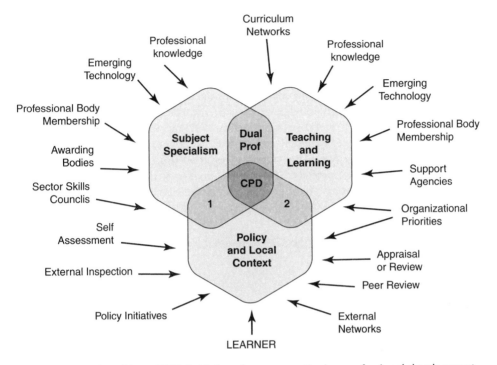

Figure 4.1 What drives CPD? Guidelines for your continuing professional development (CPD) (IfL 2009a)

Activity

Look at the indicators outlined in Figure 4.1 relating to CPD drivers. Break the components down to become more meaningful/personalized to you by either making your own map or adding further strands to the map to show specific examples (for example, policy initiatives such as Leitch (2006) or Functional Skills).

You may also wish to extend the 'Professional Body Membership' strand by adding details for the IfL and/or other professional bodies of which you are a member. You may also find it useful to identify curriculum networks and support agencies which are relevant to your specialism and context

---

Planning

A systematic approach to planning your CPD is very important, especially if you are not experienced at CPD planning/activities. By approaching CPD systematically you can then track through a reflective cycle right from the initial planning stage to impact/results stage. The IfL requires you to reflect on your CPD activities and evidence 30 hours (or pro-rata) of activity. In order to undertake this you need to critically reflect on what you have learned and how this has been applied in practice – the impact on your learners. In the previous chapter you will also have studied a variety of techniques that inform reflective practice to gain optimum benefit.

We need to consider the CPD planning model as outlined by the IfL guidelines, which is based on an 'experiential learning cycle' and has six distinct stages that need consideration annually. It is recognized that the steps do not always follow consecutively as the process is developmental and dependent on your own journey (IfL 2009a). It is likely, therefore, that some stages of the suggested process are addressed at times to suit your own particular needs. The main elements of the CPD cycle are shown in Figure 4.2. Further details regarding the process can be found on the IfL website (www.ifl.ac.uk).

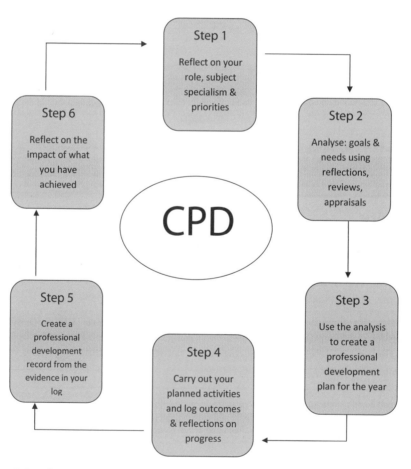

Figure 4.2 The CPD planning cycle
(Adapted from IfL 2009a)

We will consider the components listed above individually and discuss how this 6-stage planning approach can be transferred into your own professional practice. We will then go on to explore how you might identify your personal priorities, look at professional goals and needs, and how CPD might be recorded, tracked and evaluated.

Step 1: Reflect on your professional practice to date
From September 2007, a new teacher or trainer must become qualified and gain QTLS or ATLS as a priority. If you are already qualified then you must begin reflecting on the development of your professional practice by linking the LLUK standards to your role, responsibilities and classroom practice (go to www.lluk.org for further details relating to this).

Think about the national and local context in which you work and identify your key priorities to enable you to keep up to date with your subject area and to develop and improve your teaching and learning strategies.

Step 2: Carry out an analysis to identify development needs
You will need to identify and analyse your CPD priority areas using evidence from a variety of sources, such as learner feedback, evaluation, appraisals, teaching observations and your own self-assessment. For example, feedback from teaching observations might indicate a need to develop more strategies for deep learning or a need to embed employability into the curriculum (see Chapter 6).

Step 3: Create your personalized, individual development plan
After carrying out a self-assessment, you will then need to identify activities that will help you to develop as a professional. Think very carefully about the actual *type* of activity as well as the topics that are likely to be most effective for you. Your professional development plan should include a brief rationale for each activity; a time-line for achievement; outcomes and what the measures of success will be.

Step 4: Your professional development log
When you have carried out the activities identified in your plan, keep a log of those activities you have completed. The IfL's REfLECT tool is particularly useful for this. It is also a good idea to include dates in the development log along with some indication of the time spent on reflection and progress. You will also need to demonstrate in your development log the difference the activities are actually making to you, your colleagues and your learners.

Step 5: Your professional development record
It is not unusual to accumulate far more than the statutory 30 hours (or pro-rata) of development time required during the annual cycle. Most teachers in the sector will routinely undertake far more than 30 hours, much of which they don't recognize as CPD. It is suggested by the IfL (2009a) that towards the end of the annual cycle you should record the activities that have been most significant and have had the most impact on your practice. You need to demonstrate the impact of what you have achieved through your CPD.

Step 6: Reflection on practice, analysis

You need to reflect at this stage on the impact of CPD activity you have undertaken with regard not only to your own professional practice but also the impact on your colleagues and learners. This will enable you to undertake the next cycle in your development and will also be an integral part of your learning log for the current year. Your development record, when completed, will need to be sent to the IfL either through the website or by post.

Kelly (2008) suggests that the CPD activity is meaningless unless it 'makes a difference to you and your learners'. You need to put ideas into practice and analyse what you have changed, how this has affected your learners, and also gain learner feedback as part of the reflective cycle. She suggests that time spent thinking about new ideas, implementing them and undertaking a review of the outcomes all count towards your CPD hours. Of course, how you calculate the hours relies on your professional judgement or on guidelines supplied from your own organization regarding allocation of hours for activities undertaken. For instance, it may be helpful to keep notes of what you have learned from team meetings, briefings, membership events and network meetings. You will need to review advice and feedback from external assessors or awarding bodies concerning your work and discuss and plan your CPD with your manager or colleague.

Remember to keep track of your ideas. Continuing professional development is not just about attending a course, conference or workshop and it is certainly not about being 'told' what activities or events you should attend. Anything that starts you thinking about your own professional practice, whether it be an informal conversation, chance meeting with a colleague, or network meeting with peer groups is CPD (Kelly 2008). Your time plan, including measurements of success, may change as your own or organizational priorities and the wider context may change. Nevertheless, a time plan will help you to focus and possibly generate a range of different ideas as you progress through the cycle. Do keep a note of what you do throughout the year – the IfL's easy to use personal learning space for CPD, REfLECT, is free – further details relating to this tool will be discussed later in this chapter and examples will be provided of documentation used to track activities. We will also discuss some activities that you may wish to undertake as part of your CPD as there are a wide range of formal and informal activities that could count as professional development.

The IfL's *Intuition Journal* (2008b) argues that 'the very act of reflecting on and recording CPD is valuable in its own right and it demonstrates that you are always building relevant knowledge and skills in your subject or vocational area and in your teaching or training practice'. You should plan and undertake your professional development on an ongoing basis. You then need to *reflect* on what you have learnt from the activities and be able to demonstrate how the activities and reflections have made a difference to you, especially in relation to your teaching role, and then be able to show evidence of this difference.

Finally, share your plans and ideas with colleagues. Peer discussion is a very powerful tool to enable improvement, and feedback from peers is particularly developmental if it has an impact on your own practice. There may also be the opportunity to participate in joint or group CPD projects with your colleagues thus enabling reflection to take place on joint or group activities rather than individualized events.

In order to start planning your CPD, you need to first of all be able to identify your development needs. The activity outlined below will help you to do this.

Activity

Using the model of dual professionalism in Figure 4.1, you can now start to analyse your professional needs and goals in your priority areas.

Begin this process by reflecting on your practice to date. Follow the guidelines detailed in the IfL 6-step approach to reflecting on your CPD by considering specifically steps 1 and 2 in the process.

You need to look at the results of the above activity. What do they show? There are, of course, a number of ways in which you may have undertaken the task but whichever method you use, they all require honesty and a willingness to be objective. Hitching (2008) advocates the possibility of creating a 'concept map' to demonstrate your practice as a whole or simply using peer discussion as a starting point of self-reflection; some may prefer a traditional SWOT-style personal analysis of professional skills. Remember to include strengths as well as areas for improvement and use the reflective exercise as a stepping stone to ensure you understand what you are doing and why. Day (1999) argues that professional development must be 'concerned with teachers' whole selves' rather than concentrating and focusing on teaching 'skills' alone. It is important to distinguish between your development needs, as defined by context, priorities and feedback, and your development 'desires', which might be things that you really want to do but are not necessarily immediately relevant to your working context.

In order to further help you define your professional goals and needs you should evaluate and use evidence such as learner feedback, appraisals, peer review and teacher observations. You may also want to take into account external verifier reports, inspection findings and national developments which may impact on your role. The LLS is a vast arena made up of several, previously separate, sectors including further education colleges; training providers; adult and community learning; offender learning and sixth form colleges. Within the sector, individual institutions will not have precisely the same contexts and development needs and effective CPD will be related to the context and needs of each institution. While collaboration between and within institutions is fruitful and should be encouraged, we need to be cautious of the notion of 'best practice' which purports to meet universal needs.

Effective CPD

So what might 'good' or 'effective' CPD look like? As outlined above, each individual within the sector will be very different in their development route and CPD plans should be individualized and personal to the person undertaking the CPD planning and activities. However, following recent research by the TDA (2007, updated 2009), some specific guidelines have emerged as a model for consideration to help you in planning effectively for CPD activities to ensure optimum benefit for all concerned. Some of the guidelines outlined by the TDA research, *What does Good CPD Look Like? Continuing Professional Development* (2007), are discussed below – use these ideas, along with indicators already discussed, as a 'toolkit' or reference point to guide you in your CPD planning.

1 **Activity:** should be part of a long-term plan, supported by management, that gives you opportunities to apply *what* you have learned, evaluate the *effect* on your practice, and *develop* your practice. Research shows that CPD is most effective when it is part of a deliberately planned process.

2 **Planning:** a clear vision of the *effects* of improved practice should be sought. This vision is shared by those undertaking the development and by the people leading or supporting it (e.g. manager, CPD leader, peer, etc.). The plan should show what expertise, understanding or technique the CPD is intended to deliver. Clear, defined outcomes, as discussed in the planning section of this chapter, and supported by Kelly (2008), are also the starting point for being able to *evaluate* the impact of the CPD.

3 **Development of skills, knowledge and understanding** which will be practical, relevant and *applicable* to your current role or career aspirations. Continuing professional development is only effective when it is directly relevant to each participant. It is suggested that where CPD is provided for large groups, e.g. staff training events, then it would be more meaningful to separate the participants into smaller groups so the CPD may be customized to suit each type of participant.

4 **CPD training:** should be provided by relevant people – those with the necessary experience, expertise and skills – and this may sometimes be colleagues and peers. At other times they may be specialists from outside the organization such as IT specialists, subject specific specialists or teaching and learning consultants who are renowned and valued for their work in the specialized field.

5 **Lesson observation:** used as a basis for discussion about the focus of CPD and its impact. Conducted in a collaborative and non-threatening manner, observations of teaching can be extremely useful for identifying areas for development. Peer observations used in a sympathetic and developmental manner can generate a host of ideas for personal and professional development in teaching and learning.

6 **CPD models effective learning and teaching strategies:** e.g. active learning. To be effective, CPD needs to demonstrate strategies that give participants opportunities to try out ideas in a supportive setting.

7 **CPD which promotes continuous enquiry:** and problem-solving embedded in the daily life of the organization. A feature of effective CPD is an ethos in the organization of lifelong learning and development. Staff who practise CPD and regard this as an intrinsic part of their development will also act as role models for the learners.

8   **CPD impact on teaching and learning is evaluated:** and this evaluation guides subsequent professional development activities. The most effective evaluations are planned from the outset as an integral part of the
CPD.

Fairclough (2008) argues that reflection on CPD is central to the process and it is not
enough to simply log what activities have been undertaken but to also include reflective
accounts of the actual *impact* the activities have had on your professional practice and
your learners. We will be looking at effective strategies for evaluating CPD activities in
more detail later in this chapter. This is a key factor in the CPD cycle to enable review,
further planning, and measure effectiveness of the activities undertaken.

Creating your development plan

If you think about your teaching and how you plan for teaching and learning it is
evident that having clear objectives leads to more successful outcomes – you know
what you want your learners to achieve at the end of the lesson therefore you are able
to plan your teaching and learning strategies to ensure the end goals are achieved. The
importance of planning is further highlighted by Hayes et al. (2001: 28), who likened an
unplanned lesson to that of a movie with no planned script where the actors could very
well end up 'shooting the good guys instead of the bad'. In other words, good planning
is a key indicator to not only achieving successful outcomes but being able to *measure*
the effectiveness of the outcomes. By the same token, therefore, it can be said that clear
statements regarding what you desire from the professional development process will
enable you to set objectives in order to help you achieve your outcomes. For example:
'by the end of this CPD activity, I will be able to . . .'. The *type* of activity needs to be
given careful consideration and you should choose the activity that is most effective
for you. The various types of activities which can be linked to CPD are discussed in
more detail in Table 4.1 but it is important here to reiterate the concept that reflection
is not an activity that is carried out at the end of the development cycle but should be
an integral part of the process as a whole. You should reflect at the beginning, during
and at the end of the development process.

It is perhaps appropriate now to look at some of the activities you may wish to
consider as part of your CPD. The following ideas may help you in the formation of
your development plan by focusing on the activities that may be more appropriate
to your own specific needs. As previously discussed, decisions regarding specific CPD
activities can be drawn from a number of sources, as outlined by the IfL in Step 2
of the CPD cycle (see Figure 4.2), when analysing and reviewing your professional
goals and needs, including feedback based on learner appraisals, teaching observations,
your organization's own development plan and new developments in teaching and
learning.

In Table 4.1, you will see a range of activities that you may find useful as ideas
to incorporate into your own CPD plan. The list is by no means exhaustive and ideas
have been drawn from a variety of sources including the IfL (2009a), the Excellence

Table 4.1 Some suggested CPD activities

Reading relevant journals, specific items or reviewing books	Planning and running staff development events
Training courses	Organizing trips/residentials or work placements
Peer review	Public service/voluntary work
Mentoring new colleagues	Industrial placements through visits, placements, secondments or shadowing
Work shadowing	Membership of a professional body
Team teaching	Viewing and reviewing television programmes, documentaries and the internet
Peer coaching – coaching others and being coached in your subject or vocational area	Subject learning coach or advanced learning coach training
Peer observation	Curriculum design, development, validation
Carrying out and disseminating action research	Becoming an eCPD adviser or e-guide
Constructing professional dialogue/learning conversation opportunities	Peer visits to community organizations or partners
Being an active member of a committee, board, or steering group related to teaching and/or your subject area	Updating knowledge through the internet or TV. Reviewing with a group of professional colleague
Sharing ideas and resources with other colleagues and teachers – networking through REfLECT	Workshops
Attending awarding body briefings	Inset/professional development days
Accredited courses of programmes related to teacher development	Sabbaticals
Team/department/organization self-assessment	Accredited CPD courses or programmes
Reading journal articles	Examiner/assessor/verifier responsibility – disseminating this at feedback events to colleagues, etc.
Presentations at conferences, etc.	Links with employers showing impact on learning

Gateway (2009), the Training and Development Agency (2009), and the Teacher Learning Academy (2009), to name but a few. Further reading and research sources will be provided at the end of this chapter. Specific activities relating to subject specialism will be discussed in detail in Chapter 7, while ideas which underpin teaching and learning are the main focus of Chapter 6.

A personalized approach to CPD will enhance your professionalism (IfL 2009c) as you will use your own judgements and expertise to drive forward your own development ensuring activities are meaningful and relevant to your needs.

Activity

Now create your own individual development plan. You may already have a standard form issued by your organization. You may wish to use the ideas outlined in Step 3 of the 6-step approach recommended by the IfL.

What types of activities have you included and why?

In completing the above activity you should take into consideration the factors which have been previously discussed in the formation of your own development plan. Fairclough (2008) noted that you should be able to draw up your own development plan, using all the information available to you, to include 'activities, the objectives for each activity, the action plan and time-scale' not forgetting 'a column for recording *what* was achieved and what the *outcomes* were for the teacher and the learner'. Take a little time to *review* what you have completed so far. Look at the activity below and, if applicable, complete the task suggested.

Activity

Are you happy with the design of your development plan? Are you restricted in what you can use due to organizational constraints? If you feel you would like to review the design of your development plan to make it more personalized or relevant and include more meaningful activities then do so now.

As discussed previously in this chapter, it is argued that CPD is more effective when *you* personalize and take control of the process in accordance with *your* particular development needs. Observations by Ellis (2008) of the Association of Teachers and Lecturers, confirmed that CPD is often meaningless because it is often seen as a 'pick and mix of courses, . . . about meeting legislative requirements rather than professional needs . . . or it is about trying to deliver someone else's best practice'. The article supports the notion of personalized CPD by stressing the importance of priorities being agreed on an individual basis and development opportunities being 'personalized to the needs and interests of staff' while taking account of the needs of the individual, the workplace and government initiatives.

CPD case studies

In this section we will look at a number of case studies in relation to CPD, what the strengths of the activities undertaken were, why the activities were seen as successful and how the CPD activities have been used to inform future practice.

Case Study 1   Comberton Village College, Cambridgeshire

This is an 11–16 mixed comprehensive six miles west of Cambridge. In 'Every day a training day' (Martin 2006), Deputy Principal and Director of Teacher Training, Mary Martin, outlines the school's successful strategy for CPD to 'ensure that training goes well beyond the one-off event' by likening the process to a 'London Underground model for CPD' to help communicate to everyone the variety of opportunities for development available to them. Thus an 'underground map', with different coloured 'routes' was produced so staff could choose and map their own route for development from the model provided. It was found that colleagues within and external to the school used the map as a 'visual tool ... to allow them to see where they might want to journey to next'. Figure 4.3 shows the underground map developed by Comberton Village College (CVC) which clearly shows the different paths available.

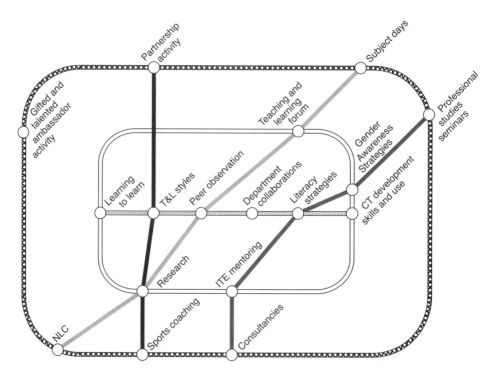

Figure 4.3   CPD 'underground' map, Comberton Village College
Key to underground map
Central Line (stipple): activities in which everyone takes part; *Circle Line* (white): next level of reflective practitioner activity; *District Line* (cross-hatch): practice can be made explicit to outsiders and offered as a model; *Victoria Line* (light grey): a route, possibly, of an advanced skills teacher; *Piccadilly Line* (dark grey): another route, possibly of someone involved in Initial Teacher Education (ITE); *Northern Line* (black): a route related to our Sports College status, for our PE/sports staff

External and internal INSET days are assessed by discussion and staff complete pro formas after taking external courses. It was found, however, that the best practice emerged from sharing ideas following internal staff training where peers could share information together formally and informally. A 'teaching and learning group' is the most popular optional discussion forum – the best teachers are 'curious about developing their practice' to enhance the experience of their pupils/students. There are several other forums including the 'department presentation and discussion forum'. Good practice resulting from the forums are often disseminated electronically via bulletin or used to 'cascade' information at other meetings.

Peer observation was found to be a powerful tool in driving CPD forward. This has now developed over the years and colleagues select peer partners, making the process more meaningful as a 'shared mutual area for exploration is agreed' before the observations are carried out. Typical areas chosen for the focus were learning styles, group work, literacy and use of ICT. Staff were recommended to keep a brief log in order to record the process and enable evaluation of the experience and outcomes.

Other successful activities include 'research community' where partnerships were formed with Cambridge University to help improve understanding of basic research methods – the aim being to build a culture where teachers improve teaching and learning through action research in their own classrooms. A video was developed using a 'critical friend' from the University to help teachers reflect on their action research experiences and how this impacted on the CPD. Some of the findings relating to the value of the research activity and its impact on professional identity were identified as 'it keeps you alive … stops you being stale … keeps you permanently on your toes … challenges you to change the status quo and take risks …', while some comments relating to the impact on teaching and learning were noted as 'it makes you assess what you are doing … makes me more aware of what's going on in my classroom … creates an open culture … the ultimate aim is to serve the needs of all individuals'. A mentor developmental model has also been at the focus of CPD and this is a driving point for all teachers in the CPD model. Some key points which emerged from the study included: show busy practitioners *how* CPD relates to everyday realities of the classroom; audit CPD needs carefully so that teachers opt in for training; provide models for professional progress; use the wealth of experience and good ideas from existing staff. See Martin (2006) for full case study.

Case Study 2   Loughborough College, Leicestershire

This is an FE college primarily for students from the age of 16 upwards but the college also has strong links with local schools and does, therefore, offer a range of programmes for some 14-year-olds. There are around 12,000 full- and part-time students. The curriculum on offer is wide ranging, from A level to vocational, including subjects such as creative media, music and hospitality and catering to name but a few. In 2009 the college celebrated its centenary, along with Loughborough University, and marked the occasion with a joint event in the Radmoor Centre, Loughborough College in September to commemorate 100 years of further and higher education in Loughborough. The college is particularly proud of its reputation for learning and excellence which was reflected in the recent independent inspections (2008). The college was awarded a 'good' rating with particular praise being given to teaching, student support and value for money. In a 2009 IQER, good practice was identified as: 'The College support for a varied and extensive programme of staff development, with its formal link to staff professional review, ensures that higher education courses are taught by well qualified and suitably trained staff' (IQER review January 2009). The college has also been awarded Investor in People status and provides a wide range of 'excellent' staff development opportunities.

In a recent interview with the Staff Development Manager, the importance of focused, relevant and effective CPD was outlined as paramount in the push for excellence. It was clear that the CPD programme and the starting point for individuals were linked explicitly with the organization's strategic plan and incorporated not only curriculum goals but also teaching and learning targets as well as staff development aims – the whole process was seen as an integrated cycle with professional teaching standards (LLUK) and the organization's priorities at the heart of the development. Monitoring of progress against CPD is undertaken in several ways including lesson observations, personal development reviews and focused action planning. A personal learning plan is developed which is focused on three main areas:

1   Subject specialism
2   Teaching and learning
3   Wider professional role – including mandatory training.

A 'learning week' is organized by staff development and mandatory events such as health and safety training are incorporated into the events organized, along with teaching and learning and other relevant training which has been identified through the professional development reviews and lesson observation summaries. The learning week had been 'very well attended and external trainers with specialized expertise were appointed for the week – there were over 100 events planned. There is also an ongoing staff development training plan throughout the year which enables individuals to target specific training needs and attend events to suit their own development.' The college's CPD recording documents have been based on the IfL REfLECT tool and staff are also encouraged to use this online facility through IfL to record and monitor their own progress. Guidelines on how to use and develop the Personal Learning Plan are available for all staff and the guidelines contain templates for both support and teaching staff to help them identify mandatory and personal development training targets.

> Staff have a clear understanding of the types of professional development available to be able to identify training needs. College priorities are also taken into account thus ensuring that dual professionalism, as identified by LLUK is incorporated into CPD planning.
> (Loughborough College Staff Development Manager)

The college is also trialling a new innovation in linking good practice to teaching and learning by appointing an 'expert teacher' in engineering to improve teaching and learning in that area. Once a review of the new role has taken place the trial will extend to other areas of the college if the pilot has been successful.

Measuring the impact of your CPD

The purpose of CPD is to make a positive impact on the teaching and learning in your organization and in your profession. Evaluating the impact of your CPD can be problematic in that it is not always easy to tell precisely which changes result from which activities. However, we can and should try to evaluate the impact of our CPD as part of learning from it and continuing it. The IfL Guidelines for CPD (IfL 2009a: 10) recommend a CPD Impact Evaluation Model which links evaluation to the reflective cycle (Table 4.2) used in identifying, planning and undertaking your CPD. This evaluation process begins at the planning stage by requiring you to establish:

- what kind of difference do I want to make and to whom?
- by when?
- what do I think the picture, evidence and data are at the outset?
- what picture and evidence do I want to achieve?

At each stage of this process you need to consider what evidence there is that change is needed; what evidence there is of your progress in planning and implementing change and what evidence there is that change has happened.

Such planning is vital to the success of CPD but you should be prepared for unexpected or unintended outcomes; these may turn out to be more valuable than the expected outcomes. There is a principle of good academic research which suggests that we constantly monitor and, if necessary, adapt our research questions, methods and purposes as the research progresses. We should not close our eyes to the possibilities and opportunities which present themselves along the way. At the end of your CPD activities you might well be implementing changes which you previously didn't even know about; a case of 'unknown unknowns'.

Evaluating CPD events

Kelly (2008), in her article *Evaluating the Impact of CPD*, explores ways of evaluating CPD other than handing out a standard questionnaire. She suggests, before any formal CPD activity takes place such as coaching, workshops, conferences, etc., that participants consider:

1   what targets or objectives the CPD activity is designed to meet;
2   what the impact of engaging in the CPD activity will be;
3   what the outcomes will be in terms of impact on classroom skills and how this will affect the learning of the students;
4   how the above can be measured;

Table 4.2 The IfL's Impact Evaluation Model

Links to the reflective cycle	CPD impact evaluation model	Examples of evidence
Steps 1 & 2 Needs and Goals	• What changes would you like to make to your practice? • How will you know when these changes have made a difference?	• Who's involved? • Expected completion date? • What changes do you want to see? • Who will be affected by these changes, e.g. learners; you; colleagues?
Steps 3 & 4 Plan and Do	• What has gone to plan and what hasn't? • Any surprises, setbacks, challenges?	**Professional Development Plan** • Reflections on the planned CPD activities • Evidence gathered on the way?
Step 5 Review and Analyse	• What worked/didn't work? • What would you have done differently if you were to do this again? • Is it too late to change anything?	• Peer discussions • Revised plan • Next steps?
Step 6 Reflection. 'So what?'	• What's changed? • What difference(s) have you made? • Have you asked the 'right' questions? • Where to now?	**Evidence of changes** • Feedback from learners; colleagues; data; documentation

Usually, evaluating the impact of a CPD event, such as a conference, is often in the form of a participant satisfaction questionnaire and while this can be valuable in recording positive or negative attitudes to the event, there are more exciting ways of evaluating impact. Kelly suggests that Guskey's five levels of impact evaluation (Guskey 2000) will help institutions to develop effective evaluation tools – as opposed to simply recording what participants thought of a particular CPD event. Guskey's five levels of impact evaluation are: (1) participant reaction; (2) participant learning; (3) organizational support and change; (4) participant use of new knowledge and skills; and (5) pupil (student) learning outcomes.

Kelly (2008) suggests questions to ask yourself in considering the five steps outlined above including sharing/cascading of CPD activities and the relationship between evaluating the actual impact; as well as misconceptions regarding the main purpose of CPD and relevance of evaluation and impact on certain groups. Different approaches for measuring and evaluating formal and informal CPD are discussed, and a pro forma regarding 'Evaluation of the impact of planned CPD activities' is also included – the pro forma may be adapted to suit individuals and institutions as required. Seven suggestions are given regarding evaluation choice:

1   learning questionnaire
2   learning discussion with line manager
3   reflective learning log
4   formally evidenced student learning outcomes with narrative
5   classroom observation and follow-up discussion
6   review of students' work
7   student interview or attitude measures, e.g. questionnaire.

Key items to include on the pro forma are shown as:

Expected teacher outcomes: What skills will you develop and how do you plan to use them? What gains in knowledge do you expect to make and how do you see this making a difference to your teaching? What do you expect to be able to do that you can't do now?

Expected student outcomes: What will be the impact on students' progress/ learning in the classroom? What are the likely time scales for this?

Measurement of student learning outcomes: How will you measure the impact of CPD on students' learning and the progress they make as a result? How will this be evidenced?

Kelly argues that allowing staff to choose the most meaningful mode of evaluation for themselves should engage them fully in the longer term outcomes and planning of CPD.

Activity   Impact evaluation

Using information from your development plan, use the impact evaluation methods discussed above to evaluate at least one CPD activity that you have undertaken recently. You may wish to consider the steps outlined by Kelly in the suggested pro forma, which lists 3 main areas as: **(1) Expected teacher outcomes, (2) Expected student outcomes, (3) Measurement of student learning outcomes,** along with an indication of your preferred evaluation choice from the seven discussed previously.

Recording and monitoring CPD

Many institutions have introduced CPD portfolios to encourage staff to appreciate the role and value of CPD – these are often referred to as 'personal CPD portfolios'. However, as the LLS is so very diverse, your institution/employer may be operating a CPD strategy that includes documents relating to performance meetings, personal development plans and recording of CPD carried out.

A TDA study (May 2008), *Establishing a Culture of Continuing Professional Development Engagement,* found that the best practice institutions did not hand out portfolios as empty 'documents' but they often contained significant information and were divided into relevant sections. For instance at the North Hertfordshire Education Support Centre, a student referral unit, each staff member's portfolio had the following structure to it:

- a job description
- staff handbook and code of conduct
- personal achievements and positive comments to recognize achievement
- training and professional development undertaken and their evaluation of it
- training undertaken
- observation reports, performance management or development reviews and references to them in Ofsted reports
- annual personal targets
- whole centre targets in which they are involved
- membership of any working parties, e.g. staff representative on line management committee or being part of the health and safety group or curriculum groups.

You need to ensure your CPD is recorded, tracked and evaluated, including forward planning for future CPD activities or actions that need to be taken forward as a result of CPD activity undertaken. The IfL suggest that you also reflect on outcomes with a colleague or group of colleagues and ask them to act as 'critical friends' as this kind of learning conversation can be powerful and support your own development process.

Many institutions are also beginning to move from paper-based portfolios to electronic versions (e-portfolios). Commercial software programs are available to purchase to enable the switch to e-portfolios to take place smoothly and some programs also allow users to print out portfolio details for those who prefer to retain a hard copy. Other schools and institutions, such as Oakwood High School, Manchester, have designed their own electronic portfolio system. The TDA study (2008) also pointed out a major drawback in e-portfolio development, perceived by many people as being the concept of 'sharing information' freely over the intranet and therefore being seen as more of a management tool rather than personal documents relating to CPD activity. Oakwood dealt with this problem by ensuring some parts of the in-house e-portfolio design maintained privacy while other sections remained public. The section recording thoughts, experiences and questions is totally private and not accessible by anyone, including managers. A set of prompts are included to help the user to think through a variety of professional development issues.

Of course, members of the IfL can use the REfLECT tool (online CPD) to help them:

- record thoughts and activities (1 year log);
- share CPD with colleagues, peers or managers for review and comment;

- plan development activities in a structured way so you think about the next steps and resources;
- count CPD hours logged.

Finally, as outlined earlier in this chapter and supported by research, it can be concluded that professional conversations and face-to-face and online discussions are vitally important as part of your ongoing development. From the onset you should aim to share your development with a colleague who will act as a critical friend, support your activity and peer review your planning and reflections on CPD. Your CPD should be personalized to suit your needs as well as the needs of your institution and will, therefore, be meaningful and relevant to your continued development in your role as a teacher/trainer.

Further resources

The IfL's REfLECT tool

REfLECT is a personal learning space secure and private to each member. You can choose any method to plan and record your CPD – your employer may have a preferred system that you can use. Further details are available from the IfL website (www.ifl.ac.uk). Log onto the members' area and click on the REfLECT link.

5 CPD for the new teacher

...inexperience is an asset to be exploited. It is of use, however, only in the context of participation, when supported by experienced practitioners who both understand its limitations and value its role.

(Lave and Wenger 1991: 117)

This chapter is about:

- What new and recently qualified teachers in the LLS need
- Induction of new teachers
- Appraisal
- The developmental journey of teachers in the LLS
- From initial teacher training (ITT) to CPD
- Career routes for new teachers in the lifelong learning sector

This chapter is intended not only as a guide and resource for new teachers in the lifelong learning sector but also as a guide for managers who want to retain and develop new staff for the benefit of the teacher, the organization and, above all, the learners. Staff are an expensive commodity and it is worth investing time, and money, in their induction and early development.

It has been estimated that there are approximately 300,000 people working in the LLS, and that many of these will retire by 2020.

Thompson (2009: 1) suggests that: '20 percent of further education teaching staff will hit 65, the statutory retirement age, in the next ten years. Shuffle down the age groups to, say, 45 and half of all FE teachers will be picking up their free bus passes by 2029'. Such major demographic shifts within the sector have implications beyond simply recruiting new teachers to replace retiring teachers, but for the whole question of succession planning and recruiting people who will become not only teaching and learning professionals but also managers and leaders.

Alongside the current emphasis on the sector to train and retrain people made redundant by the economic downturn; the implementation of Diplomas requiring new skills sets of teachers across a wider sector including schools; and the raising of the school leaving age, it seems likely that many new jobs will be created in the sector and the range of teaching and training roles will broaden. Recent indications suggest that the LLS will continue to be affected by funding limitations; however, large numbers of new teachers continue to join the profession, and many career changers are attracted to the concept of sharing their skills, particularly through the LLUK's Catalyst programme.

What do new and recently qualified teachers need?

New teachers join the LLS through many varied routes and bring a wealth of different skills, experience and knowledge, often of specific trades and occupations vital to the skills agenda. Along with these important skills they also have, however, a wide range of individual and personal development needs. Managers who fail to meet the needs of these people risk high staff turnover, unstable departments, staff absenteeism, and a poor student learning experience, which then affects retention, achievement, inspection and, therefore, funding. To be successful colleges and learning providers need to attract, retain and develop a skilled and talented, as well as responsive and adaptable, workforce.

The lifelong learning sector workforce is very diverse; this is both a strength and a challenge. As well as new entrants coming from trades and professions, many new teachers will come through university with subject and vocational qualifications and train full time or part time to achieve teaching qualifications and develop their CPD. Given these different levels of previous achievement, culture, work ethic and expectations, what constitutes the most appropriate training and professional development? All new teachers in the sector are now required to gain a recognized teaching qualification (CTLLS or DTLLS according to the teaching role). This was not always the case, as Simmons and Thompson (2007: 171) point out: 'Although college staff usually held qualifications in their own field of expertise, it was not unusual for them to teach without either a Cert Ed or PGCE.' Given the obligation to gain such a qualification, what else do new teachers need to join and flourish within the sector? During 2007–8 a small-scale research study was carried out with teachers who had qualified at the University of Derby to find out what help and support they needed during their first appointment to a teaching post. The study included both full time, pre-service students, and part time in-service students, across the partnership of four colleges. Although the research question was kept open, we were not surprised to find that their needs were very individual, but they did fall broadly into three categories:

1   what new teachers need
2   what everyone new in post needs
3   what teachers, experienced, but newly qualified, need.

Activity

- What do you think might be differences between these groups?
- Do you think these categories reflect your own experiences?
- When you were just starting as a teacher or in a new post, what support did you need? To what extent did you get it?

New in post

This refers to those who have a history of employment in the sector but have taken up a new post in another institution, or a promotion within their current institution, and includes everyone up to heads of department and principals. When you are new to the job there are certain institutional things you need to know so that you can function effectively in your new environment. If staff are to settle in quickly, enjoy the job and know what they are doing and what is expected of them, then they need to be properly inducted into the role. It is also vital to realize that they cannot possibly retain all this new information so they need a manual to refer to in some format and a mentor or buddy for the things that are not in the manual, and reassurance. If the institution is the same and you have just moved role or department induction may be a fairly straight-forward activity, involving a 'handover' from the previous post holder, but it may also be a challenge in that it requires the development of different working relationships with existing colleagues.

What do new teachers need?

It has been suggested that, 'The inexperienced young teacher is the most valuable investment that a school can have in future achievement and success' (Burgess 2001: 84). A new teacher is a significant investment for an organization and if this person is not supported as they become part of the organization then the investment is, to some extent, wasted. It is essential that new teachers are treated as an asset and are supported by experienced professionals, rather than seen as a burden to be carried until they are experienced.

In Chapter 1 we considered the notion of a college or learning provider as a learning organization and the induction of new teachers and teachers new in post should, ideally, be considered as inductions into learning communities. It is a crucial time in which new recruits require support and guidance if they are to become part of a team that works and learns together. Lave and Wenger refer to social settings in which learning takes place in the context of shared goals and activities as 'communities of practice'. Our workplaces are communities of practice, or learning communities, which are strange and unusual at first but entering them involves moving from the periphery to the centre and becoming professionals within that setting.

The experienced 'new' teacher

It is only recently that there has been a requirement that all teachers and trainers in the LLS should be appropriately qualified to teach. In the 1990s it was not uncommon for a teacher to be appointed by a college with the proviso that they would undertake teacher training as a condition of their employment; this condition was not always met and the numbers of qualified staff were not comprehensively monitored. As a consequence teacher trainers were sometimes confronted with trainees, often colleagues, who were reluctant, even hostile, to the requirement that they should undertake a Cert Ed or a City and Guilds programme. In many cases new teachers came into the sector from industry or business and their subject specialism was seen, rightly, as their most valuable asset. We now recognize that even the most highly qualified and skilled subject specialist is not necessarily going to be a good teacher and that they will need training and support in the basics of producing schemes of work, lesson planning and a variety of learning techniques as well as a good theoretical underpinning of teaching and learning.

In our small-scale research study, teachers with more than two years' actual teaching experience, but in their first year post qualification as a teacher felt they needed:

- additional subject training
- vocational up-skilling or practice
- mentor training
- observation of other teachers in their own subject area
- teaching technologies
- management development.

The induction of new teachers

Every educational institution will have an induction programme. Such programmes, however, vary tremendously in scope and effectiveness. Anecdotal evidence suggests that lip service is often paid to the process and it is little more than a tour of premises; an introduction to a few key people; the provision of a handbook; and the identification of a mentor who may, or may not, be willing to support the newcomer. The checklist in Table 5.1 is based on the authors' experience in teaching and managing in FE colleges for many years and is intended to act as a guide to what you should expect from your induction.

The two elements in the induction checklist match the notion of the 'dual professional' which is the foundation for development as recognized by the IfL. For many working in the sector the driving force is their subject specialism because this is the basis of their expertise, even passion, and what brought them into the job. However, when in post new teachers have a professional obligation to develop the theory and practice of teaching and learning as well as to keep up to date with developments in their subject. In addition, teachers in the sector may be asked to teach a broader range of students and to be flexible and adaptable in what they teach. For example, English teachers should not necessarily expect to teach only at A level; they may reasonably be asked to contribute to functional skills programmes. It is important, however, that teachers are flexible but don't find themselves being required to teach something that they have little experience of; this is bad for the learners and the organization. The two elements of the 'dual professional' are examined in detail in Chapter 6 (CPD for teaching and learning) and Chapter 7 (Subject-specific CPD).

Appraisal and performance management

Appraisals are, or should be, an essential element of supporting the development of new and existing teachers and they are usually held with a person's line manager at

Table 5.1 Induction checklist for new teachers and teachers new in post

General institutional	Subject specific
Employer 'who's who' list	Timetable
Telephone list	Information on your groups
Maps of the site/s	Specifications for your teaching
Institutional structure	Assessment policy
Departmental structure	Schemes of work
Administrative support	Lesson plans and formats
Resources available and where to find them	Subject specific resources and where to find them/book them out
Photocopying systems and paper access	Access to classroom ICT and what is available (and training if you need it)
IT access, internet and intranet, policies and procedures	Team information, meeting schedules, training etc.
Basics: toilets, car parking, hours of work etc.	Partner organizations, policy and protocols
Health and Safety policies and training required, self checking systems	Classroom risk assessments and policies
Job description	Teaching/Learning/Assessment policy
Professional development details, and recording system	Working at Home arrangements
Appraisal system and policy	Intranet and subject resources, notices, discussion groups, Wikis, etc., and policy monitoring
Probationary period and policy	CPD arrangements, and access to information
Library access and opening times	Subscriptions to journals
Telephone access	Conferences, trips, and fieldwork with students, and policies
Where you will be working and equipment required	Absence policy, who do you inform?
Financial information and regulations about ordering and allowances	Tutorial arrangements
Budget policy	Register policy and practices
Grievance or disciplinary policies	Examination arrangements
Student support policies and contacts	Handing in work policy, turnaround and feedback protocols
Complaints procedures	Sharing classes? Who does what?
Equality and diversity policy and support	Discipline policy and practice
Marketing contacts and processes	Homework policy and practice
Induction to job, department and institution	Storage of your materials, paper or paperless?
Driving for work and other travel arrangements	Policy regarding classroom displays
Quality processes and policies	Referencing policy (always a sensitive subject!)
Who do you ask?	Who your mentor is?

regular meetings set by the organization's human resources function. The appraisal is usually based on a review of the appraisee's development, progress and career plans and sets individual targets within the context of the aims of the organization. Since the introduction of the IfL's requirement for all teachers to undertake a minimum of 30 hours of CPD, many colleges combine appraisals with a review and discussion of the teacher's CPD plans and use these as a basis for an ongoing individual learning and development plan. Early appraisal and the agreement of a development plan should be part of induction and are central to the development and retention of new teaching staff. While recognizing the organization's need to set goals and engage staff in meeting them, appraisal and CPD planning should, as far as possible, avoid imposing development activities and recognize that teachers are best placed to make judgements and decisions about their own CPD needs, especially relating to improving teaching and learning.

The concept of 'performance management and review' takes a slightly different perspective from appraisal in that it is based on the notion of shared responsibility for performance and dialogue between manager and staff. Performance management:

> rejects the cultural assumption that only managers are accountable for the performance of their teams and replaces it with the belief that responsibility is shared between managers and team members. In a sense, managers should regard the people who report to them as customers for the managerial contribution and services they provide.
>
> (Armstrong 2003: 481)

The concept of performance development and review helps us make links to CPD through reflective practice. Every task that people undertake and every experience they have presents them with a learning opportunity and part of performance management is about managing continuous learning. In dialogue with managers and team leaders individuals can reflect on, and are helped to reflect on, what they have done and draw conclusions as to their future development and CPD activities. Key to successful performance and review is that participants should respect each others' professionalism; managers should recognize teachers as professionals who are in the best place to know what is needed for their own learners and to improve teaching and learning. Reviews are not 'top-down' appraisals in which the reviewee feels guided, or cajoled, into particular conclusions. As Armstrong points out, performance reviews:

> should be more like 'free-flowing' open meetings where views are exchanged so that agreed conclusions can be reached. A performance review should be regarded as a conversation with a purpose, which is to reach firm and agreed conclusions about the individual's development
>
> (Armstrong 2003: 496)

Induction – a case study

Following her first class degree in psychology and completion of a pre-service DTLLS qualification, Jane started work as a part-time teacher of psychology at a large FE college. Although a new, inexperienced teacher in a new area, she loved her subject and was keen to begin her career in teaching and eventually, she planned, management.

On her first day, the head of department took Jane into a crowded social sciences and humanities staffroom and gave a general introduction to all the teachers then present. She introduced Jane to her mentor who, after a brief 'hello' had to rush off – Jane didn't see her again for two days. The induction handbook appeared to be cobbled together from a variety of sources and was difficult to navigate. She hadn't even been shown where the toilets were or where she could get a cup of coffee. There was clearly tension in the staffroom. Comments concerning the gender and ability of Jane's mentor were muttered with accompanying sniggers. Members of staff in other departments, especially vocational, were hostile to the department, which they considered academic and irrelevant to the 'real world'.

Jane applied herself to her teaching. Her students were generally well behaved and well motivated. Some had behavioural issues and some, it became clear, had specific learning difficulties. Jane's induction gave little information about how she could support these students.

In spite of these challenges, Jane's students had the best retention and achievement for that academic year; this was not appreciated by all her colleagues. At the end of the year a permanent job became available which, to the surprise of her manager, Jane didn't apply for. Very soon after, she gained a full-time post in another college and eventually became head of psychology.

Discussion

What can we learn from this case study, particularly concerning induction of new staff; mentoring and mentor training; appraisal and CPD?

The developmental journey of the new teacher in the LLS

The journey metaphor is useful in helping to understand and conceptualize the experience of the new teacher. The beginning of a journey is a time of anticipation and excitement but also anxiety; the destination of the journey is probably known but the route and the scenery are largely unknown. Induction, support and mentoring can reassure the new teacher on their journey, especially when they encounter unfamiliar situations, new colleagues, managers and students or when they feel that they have failed in some way or not met expectations. Good mentoring and support will help new recruits to understand that they will encounter problems, make errors and occasionally feel like giving in, but that these are part of everyone's development. Becoming a reflective practitioner (see Chapter 3) is the basis for all improvement and for understanding the developmental journey, as well as the starting point of CPD. There are several other theories and ideas which can help trainees and mentors to understand the developmental process, some of which are outlined below.

Help! to second nature

Reynolds (1965) suggested a model of developing competence for use with social work trainees. The stages of this model are:

1   Help!
2   Have a go
3   Hit and miss
4   'Sound'
5   Relative mastery
6   Second nature

If we take learning to drive a car as context for this model, most of us can recall the dread we felt on first sitting behind the wheel and struggling with clutch control and carrying out several other operations simultaneously. Through repeated attempts and supported practice we become confident drivers to whom all the difficult coordination of controls and skills become second nature. Much of our skills and knowledge will, like driving a car, become second nature but we must ensure that 'second nature' doesn't become complacency. Success in teaching and learning requires us to challenge and develop our practice by regular reflection, review and learning. During this process we need the guidance and support, and occasionally the discipline, of a sensitive instructor. For the new teacher mentors, colleagues and managers need to provide similar guidance and support.

From 'novice' to 'expert'

Berliner (2001) provides a framework for conceptualizing teacher development from 'novice' to 'expert'. The novice teacher is the raw recruit who is learning the basics and is relatively inexperienced and inflexible; the 'expert' is like the racing driver or professional footballer who is at one with their art, performing effortlessly and intuitively. Experience and length of service do not necessarily make an expert; experience needs reflection if we are to become expert teachers. The main features of each stage are:

Stage 1: novice

The beginner tends to be relatively inflexible and to follow rules and procedures or guidelines provided by others. At this stage the immediacy of the 'real-world' experienced as isolated episodes tends to guide their actions.

Stage 2: advanced beginner

At this stage the teacher is starting to think beyond isolated episodes of experience and to recognize similarities of occurrence and experience; they are starting to make sense of their experience.

Stage 3: competent

At this stage teachers are starting to make conscious choices about what they are going to do. They are becoming more autonomous and set priorities and decide plans but have the confidence to adjust them as appropriate. They may not yet be as fast, fluid and flexible as their more experienced colleagues.

Stage 4: proficient

At this stage teachers have developed a bank of practice and theory upon which they can reflect and a holistic understanding of teaching and learning. Know-how and intuition have become more important and effective performance has become 'second nature'. Berliner (2001: 23) writes of 'the micro-adjustments made in learning to ride a bicycle – at some point, individuals no longer think about these things. They develop an "intuitive" sense of the situation.'

Stage 5: expert

Berliner suggests that many teachers will never become experts in the real sense of the word but those that do have an almost arational and non-analytical approach to their practice, performing effortlessly and fluidly. When things are going well they do not analyse or deconstruct experience but when they encounter problems they can be reflective and analyse and evaluate their performance. Malcolm Gladwell in his book *Outliers* (2008) suggests that it takes 10,000 hours of practice to make an expert!

Communities of practice

This concept was developed by Lave and Wenger (1991) based on studies of how people learn in apprenticeships. In apprenticeships learning is mainly a process of socialization in which people begin their experience by observing others and performing simple tasks and gradually, as knowledge and experience deepen, they take on more complex tasks until they become integrated into the 'community of practice' – a group sharing common interests, goals and a desire to learn.

There are some implications for the induction and development of new teachers in this theory. While it may be impractical, and expensive, to allow a new teacher simply to observe and undertake simple tasks, we need to be aware of the dangers of throwing someone 'in at the deep end' and expecting them to take on the same quantity and complexity of work as their existing colleagues. This applies, perhaps to a lesser extent, to someone new in post who has performed a similar role in another organization.

From teacher experience to abstract concepts

This model of the teacher's developmental journey was developed by one of the authors as part of a small-scale research project based on feedback from new teachers and experienced but unqualified teachers on ITT courses with a wide range of service histories and sector engagements (Pickering 2008). The research, and the model, suggests that teachers begin in the 'teacher experience zone', move through the 'applied concepts zone' and then into the 'abstract concepts zone' (see Figure 5.1). As they gain experience they make return visits to the different zones when dealing with new demands or problems, such as new specifications, new technology or new groups of students.

The teacher experience zone
New teachers begin in this zone and their time in it may vary according to the support and mentoring they receive. This is similar to Berliner's (see above) 'novice' zone where immediate experience is the main influence.

The applied concepts zone
Experience together with teacher training and CPD help the new teacher into this zone where they start to see the bigger picture of their work and the context in which it takes place. Supported by mentors and their own reflective practice they start to apply theory to practice and analyse their performance.

The abstract concepts zone
This zone is similar to Berliner's 'proficient' and 'expert' categories. The teacher is now confident in their profession and has a firm foundation of skills and

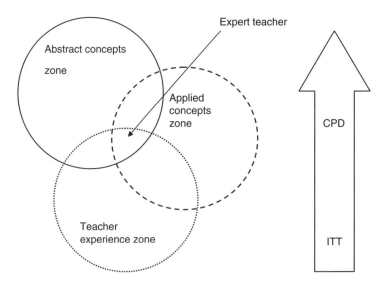

Figure 5.1 The developmental journey of the new teacher in the lifelong learning sector

experience. In this zone they can theorize about their work and consider and plan for new developments.

The most important implication of this model is that it recognizes that teachers do not become experts and stay experts in all contexts. Experienced teachers are able to move freely between the zones; CPD guides and supports their journey. There is also a link here to reflective practice (see Chapter 3) in that experienced teachers will recognize when they are revisiting the 'teacher experience' and 'applied concept' zones and seek out appropriate CPD.

Activity

Consider the three zones: teacher experience; applied concepts; and abstract concepts.

- In which zone do you consider yourself to be now?
- To what extent does this model reflect your own experience?
- If you are an 'experienced' teacher, were there times when you returned to the first zones?
- How does it feel to return to the 'teacher experience' zone?
- What support and guidance do you need when you return to those zones?

From ITT to CPD

ITT and CPD are not separate activities but need to be formally linked so that the latter builds explicitly on the former.

(Coffield 2008: 23)

The period of initial teacher training is where good CPD habits should begin. Training courses for the LLS generally require the trainees to produce an individual (or initial) learning plan (ILP) which will become the basis of reflection and CPD. Your ILP can be considered as the starting point of reflection and of your CPD. It can take the form of an audit of your existing knowledge, skills, attitudes and personal qualities; to identify your strengths and to highlight any uncertainties you have about becoming a teacher in the lifelong learning sector. It is most likely that your course tutors will provide an ILP format which you will be expected to use as an initial audit, but also as a document to refer to during tutorials and as a measure of the distance you have travelled at the end of your course. The important point is to use the ILP to kick-start your CPD, not merely something you produce because you've been asked to.

If you haven't been provided with an ILP pro forma, here are a few areas you might wish to consider for your development. You can develop a rating scale for these so that you can see your starting point and the distance travelled.

What do you know about or how confident are you about the following?

- the roles and responsibilities of a teacher
- planning a course
- planning a session
- how people learn
- Skills for Life and Key Skills
- communication skills
- presentation skills
- demonstration skills
- questioning and explaining
- using a range of teaching and learning methods
- designing and using resources
- using ICT
- health and safety
- assessing learning
- reflection
- equality, inclusion and diversity
- subject knowledge and skills
  - how up to date are you?
  - latest ideas in teaching and learning
  - sources of information
  - subject specialist professional development

An ILP is important because it makes clear from the outset that CPD is an individual process in which each teacher is best placed to make judgements and decisions regarding their CPD based on their own needs, the needs of their learners, the needs of the organization and the context of the sector.

Career routes for new teachers in the lifelong learning sector

People entering the sector as new teachers have a wide variety of experience, motivation and plans for their career development. Good management and performance review will, working with the new entrant, begin to identify teachers' motivations and goals and help them to achieve them in the context of the organization. Many teachers, in all sectors of education, say that they feel undervalued in the work they do in the front line while their managers, like generals, issue instructions from a safe distance. The term 'delivery staff' is often used to describe teachers. As we point out elsewhere in this book teachers are more than just 'deliverers' of packages of learning; they are professionals who understand their learners and their needs and goals and plan, teach and develop accordingly. If teaching and learning is at the heart of what we do, we need to value and support teachers as the people who make this happen. Having said this, colleges and learning organizations need skilled and talented managers who can create the structures and the ethos necessary for the managerial and financial success of the college as well as nurturing good teaching and learning and high achievement. Put simply, there are two main career paths in the sector – teaching and management.

Teaching route

There is much to be said in favour of an enhanced career structure for teachers whereby they can have increasing responsibility for the planning and the development of the curriculum as well as the improvement of teaching and learning. This has been tried, with varying levels of commitment and success, in a number of FE colleges which offer advanced practitioner status as 'learning directors' or 'learning managers'. It seems a shame that teachers, as with so many other professions such as social work, feel that progression and promotion take them further away from what they came into the profession to do. At present career possibilities for teachers in the LLS seem to be the following:

- advanced practitioner status, where it is available;
- becoming a Subject Learning Coach (SLC) or Advanced Learning Coach (ALC) (these routes are discussed in Chapter 7, 'Subject-specific CPD');
- subject specialist;
- subject specialist mentor;
- staff development and teacher training;
- student support and guidance roles;
- specific support, for example, with learning difficulties and disability (LDD);
- pastoral and/or academic support and guidance;
- team leader with teaching and some managerial responsibility. This could be regarded as a kind of 'half-way' house between teaching and management.

Other routes which keep teachers mainly in teaching and learning but may take them out of college, include: teaching and learning consultancy; staff development in business; moving into higher education.

Management route

A full discussion of management routes and opportunities is beyond the scope of this book, suffice to say that potential managers might be spotted early and appropriate CPD agreed with them. Increasingly, if you choose the management route you will need to undertake formal training and gain relevant qualifications and experience.

It is important to consider the kind of manager you would like to be and, as an experienced teacher, you will probably have some ideas about how you would like to have been managed. One of the main messages of this book is that managers and teachers need to respect each others' professionalism and work cooperatively to meet the organization's mission and objectives. Suggested readings and sources of information for those interested in following a management route are given below.

Further reading and sources of information

Briggs, A. (2006) *Middle Management in FE*. London: Continuum.
Collins, D. (2006) *Survival Guide for College Managers and Leaders*. London: Continuum.
Jameson, J. (2008) *Leadership in Post Compulsory Education*. London: David Fulton.
Jameson, J. (2007) *Ultimate FE Leadership and Management Handbook*. London: Continuum.

Websites

Association of College Managers (ACM)

The ACM website offers a number of useful publications related to management which you can download free without becoming a member. http://www.acm.uk.com/

Institute of Leadership and Management (ILM)

The ILM offers a wide range of courses for aspiring managers, many of which will be suitable for those working in the LLS.

Their 'Qualification finder' helps you refine your search. http://www.i-l-m.com/learn-with-ilm.aspx

Learning and Skills Improvement Service (LSIS)

This offers a wide range of support and programmes, including

- From Management to Leadership
- Aspiring Principals and Senior Leadership Programme
- Leadership Development Framework

http://www.lsis.org.uk/Services/ProgrammesServices/Pages/default.aspx

Training and Development Agency (TDA)

Performance management.
http://www.tda.gov.uk/teachers/performance_management.aspx

UCU (Universities and Colleges Union)

The UCU provides a wide range of support, guidance and benefits for members in colleges and universities. www.ucu.org.uk

Their *Early Careers Guide* is an extremely useful introduction to working in FE and HE. Because it's produced by the union it contains important advice and information on contracts, as well how to get help if you experience harassment or bullying. http://www.ucu.org.uk/index.cfm?articleid=4550

You should also check out the website for a wide range of publications and sources of support.

6 CPD for teaching and learning

> As you reflect on your teaching practice, listening to the many and varied sources of feedback on your performance, **you** are best placed to determine the type and nature of activities that will make the greatest impact on teaching and learning.
>
> IfL (2009a) *Guidelines for your continuing professional development (CPD)*
> (emphasis added)

This chapter is about:

- How has the learning and teaching context changed in recent years?
- What is effective learning and teaching in the lifelong learning sector?
- Brief review of learning theories
- Models and principles of effective learning
- Some suggested themes and topics for CPD in learning and teaching
- Sources of information and further reading and research

Changing contexts

The IfL Guidelines for CPD remind us of the importance of understanding shifting policy contexts and priorities at organizational, local and national level. Understanding these contexts is relevant to teaching and learning because we will be challenged, even required, to adapt and develop our teaching in response to new groups of learners and new courses of learning, for example the Diplomas. The following is a very brief recap of some relevant contextual issues.

We are said to be living in a 'knowledge society' or 'knowledge economy' where constant change will be the main feature of people's lives, especially their working lives. The 'job for life' culture has long since disappeared; in the 'Shift Happens' video (UK version http://www.youtube.com/watch?v=QeoKQbT8BKs) we are told that the US Labor Department estimates that by the age of 38 today's learners will have had between 10 and 14 different jobs. Will these current and future learners need to be filled with increasingly vast bodies of content or will they need to learn in ways which will encourage and develop their learning skills?

The 14–19 agenda and associated developments such as the new Diplomas and the requirement to stay in education or training until 18 represent the response to the UK's poor staying on rates and the concern about those who fall into the not in education, employment or training (NEET) category. Learners who have not been engaged with traditional schooling methods and content are unlikely to engage with the same again, just in a different place.

The relationship between education and the economy has long been a topic of debate. This issue has become centre stage with the skills agenda, particularly through the Leitch Report (Leitch 2006). Quite what is meant by 'skills' is not always clear but we can be sure that it includes literacy and numeracy. The new Functional Skills are a top priority for all learners and teachers – this means all teachers. The Minimum Core makes clear that all teachers have a responsibility for supporting the development of literacy and numeracy. To this end teachers in the sector are required to have literacy and numeracy at a minimum of Level 2 and to be familiar with the framework of Functional Skills. Most importantly, the Minimum Core is about removing barriers to learning and understanding by developing inclusive learning practices. This requires understanding of the ways in which people learn and the development of a wide repertoire of teaching and learning methods.

As well as Functional Skills we need to develop learners' thinking skills and our ability to provide programmes of learning which have regular opportunities for learners to develop higher-order cognitive skills and abilities. These are best developed when learners are challenged and engaged with problems to solve as well as content to digest.

Most importantly, young people entering the lifelong learning sector now will have lived all of their lives within a digital universe where the use of mobile phones, social networking sites, texts and the whole panoply of digital devices and experiences are central not just to their learning but to their lives. Older people might bemoan these developments and what they believe to be their negative effects, such as short attention spans. We can encourage learners to engage with more 'traditional' forms of learning – the lesson, the lecture – but we can't, neither should we seek to, change their fundamental ways of being. There is evidence to suggest that popular culture and digital technology are not responsible for 'dumbing down' in the way that many people assume. Steven Johnson, in his book *Everything Bad is Good for You* (Johnson 2006) argues persuasively that popular culture provides cognitive enrichment. Marshall (2007: 105) suggests that FE teachers should engage with the new technology and that it 'deserves our serious, creative and sustained attention'. Marshall, however, strikes a cautionary note based on reviewing relevant studies on learning and the impact of ICT: 'We know from these studies that, on its own, ICT does not transform standards of provision. So it seems that any strategy for change in FE must account for the wide range of factors that contribute to quality in learning' (Marshall 2007: 103). It's easy to be seduced by the 'gee-whizz' nature of ICT, but Marshall's comment reminds us that there is no single magic bullet that can transform learning.

All the above developments are underpinned by a shift in emphasis from teaching to learning and the development of lifelong learners. This applies to teachers as much as it does to learners. Teachers are lifelong learners, developing their subject-specific and pedagogical skills. This call for continuing development can easily be seen as an extra chore in the very busy lives of teachers in the lifelong learning sector, but learning new ways can often make your work more enjoyable and, sometimes, easier. As Scales (2008: 4) suggests: 'If you're not learning, you're not teaching very well. Not only will you lack up to date skills and knowledge, you will have little to enthuse you and, consequently, your learners.'

A brief review of learning theories

In order to provide a fuller understanding of what constitutes effective learning and teaching in the lifelong learning sector it is necessary to briefly revisit some theories of learning. Teachers will find it difficult to reflect on and improve their practice without some theoretical underpinning: 'An understanding of theory is essential for teaching in post-compulsory education and training. However, it is most useful and more readily understood when it is put into practice' (Scales 2008: 57).

In his book on teaching in university John Biggs suggests three levels of thinking about teaching and learning which are also relevant to teaching in the lifelong learning sector. The three levels are:

1   *What the learner is* – on this level of understanding the responsibility for learning, or not, is seen to be the learner's. It fits with theories of fixed ability (see Claxton 2002; Hart et al. 2004 for criticism of 'fixed ability'). The teacher's role is to transmit content; those learners who understand it do so, this model suggests, because they have ability. Those who don't understand it don't have ability. It's a kind of 'blame the student' model. You might still encounter one or two 'old-timers' in the sector who suggest that they find it difficult to teach present-day students because they are not 'as good as they used to be'.

2   *What the teacher does* – this level of understanding is more positive in that it stresses the role of the teacher in improving their teaching. It's about widening the range of teaching and learning techniques and improving effectiveness in order to 'get the message across' more effectively. This level, however, still lacks a coherent theory of how people learn.

3   *What the learner does* – this level is more student centred and encourages teachers to understand how learners learn and how they can help them. It is based on constructivist theory which suggests that learning cannot merely be transmitted or 'delivered' to learners; they have to create their own understanding and connect it to what they already know.

(Biggs and Tang 2007: 16–19)

Behaviourism

Behaviourism developed, largely, from the experimental work of B.F. Skinner and E.L. Thorndike based on a variety of animals. The theory is concerned with observable changes in behaviour and suggests that we learn in response to external stimuli. Changes in behaviour result from reward and reinforcement or from negative sanctions; this theory has little concern for cognition and understanding. Apart from brief discussions, behaviourism is largely absent from the discourse of learning theory. McLay et al. (2010: 88) assert that behaviourism 'diminishes the richness of learning', although they suggest that we shouldn't dismiss it completely as it offers some insights into how the role of reward, in the form of praise and achievement, can positively benefit learning. Behaviourism can also offer insights into the origins of some learners' fears and anxieties.

Constructivism

This theory underpins Biggs's (see above) ideas about learning and teaching. Constructivism holds that learning is a process of mental construction whereby new learning is connected to what we already know and our mental frameworks adjust and develop. In this theory learners need help to construct frameworks for learning. It is connected to the notion of 'deep learning'. As Biggs suggests, 'Teaching is not a matter of transmitting but of engaging students in active learning, building their knowledge in terms of what they already understand' (Biggs and Tang 2007: 21).

The Russian psychologist Lev Vygotsky (1896–1934), stressed the sociocultural aspects of constructivism and believed that children learn first on a social level by interacting with others and then on an individual level (see Woolfolk et al. 2008: 52).

Deep and surface learning

When learners build their own knowledge and understanding in a constructivist way they are more likely to retain this and to understand it in a deep way. Deep learners construct frameworks of knowledge and understanding; they make connections and recognize underlying principles. Deep learning tends to be lasting learning, in contrast to surface learning which is characterized by rote learning, memory and lower level cognitive activities. The challenge for teachers, then, is to develop deep learners. The key to this is using a wider range of learning and teaching activities which require higher level cognition, such as case studies and problem-based learning (see later discussion in Themes and Topics for CPD, p. 95).

Humanism

Humanism is about removing barriers to learning and creating a safe and secure learning environment. It is underpinned by the simple principle that we all need to feel good about ourselves and to develop positive self-esteem. One of the key figures in this area is Carl Rogers (1902–1987) who worked mainly in counselling and psychotherapy but provides much useful advice for learning and teaching.

Brain-based and lessons from neuroscience

Recent developments in research in understanding the brain, particularly the use of Magnetic Resonance Imaging (MRI), have increased our understanding even though it is still at an early stage. For many educationalists and psychologists 'brain-based' learning is contentious and a number of brain-based approaches, for example 'Brain Gyms', have become popular but have little neuroscientific evidence to support them. However, it now seems clear that the brain's 'plasticity' means that it can adapt and develop throughout life: 'The brain's continuing plasticity suggests that it is well designed for lifelong learning and adaptation to new situations and experiences, and such adaptation can even bring about significant changes in its structure' (Teaching and Learning Research Programme n.d.: 9). Blakemore and Frith (2005) present an excellent overview of recent research into the brain's development at various stages of life.

Situated learning

Situated learning theory suggests that skills and knowledge are learned within particular settings, such as the workplace. Woolfolk et al. (2008: 414–15) state that:

> Situated learning emphasises that learning in the real world is not like studying in school. It is more like an apprenticeship where novices, with the support of an expert guide and model, take on more and more responsibility, until they are able to function independently.

These authentic settings in which there are shared goals and activities can be described as 'communities of practice' (Lave and Wenger 1990). Even if the situation is not real it can be more meaningful to learners if there is a simulated situation or some attempt to make the learning relevant and meaningful to learners.

Learning styles

Teachers in all sectors have become familiar with and use learning styles of one kind or another. The most widely used are VAKT (visual, auditory, kinaesthetic and tactile), Kolb's learning cycle and Honey and Mumford's variant of Kolb. (You can read more about these from the references below.) The problem with learning styles is that there are so many different versions of them. The report *Should We Be Using Learning Styles?* (Coffield et al. 2004) identifies more than 70 different learning styles models; many of these are tied to expensive packages of materials and training. Coffield et al.'s report suggests that there is little to be gained from labelling learners as, for example, 'visual learners' or 'kinaesthetic learners'. A valuable CPD activity may be to research learning styles and review your use of them. The most useful message we can take from learning styles is that people learn in many ways and, consequently, teachers need to develop a wide repertoire of teaching and learning activities.

Coffield particularly singles out VAKT for criticism and he is worth quoting at length, if only to get a feel of the passion with which he expresses his views.

> There is **no** scientific justification for teaching and learning strategies based on VAKT and tutors should **stop** using learning style instruments based on

them. There is **no** theory of VAKT from which to draw **any** implications for practice. It should be a dead parrot. It should have ceased to function.
(Coffield 2008: 32, original emphasis)

What is effective learning?

Traditional ideas about teaching and learning

Despite advances in teaching and learning, some 'traditional' ideas still exist where teaching is seen as something that teachers do to students; that it entails an all-knowing teacher 'filling up empty buckets' (the students) with information and content. The current focus on testing, particularly in schools, tends to reinforce this notion. We suggest that this model of teaching and learning is outdated and unsuited to the needs of the twenty-first century. In particular, we would argue that effective teaching entails a move away from the model of teaching as transmission of content from teachers to learners. Educational discourse has become saturated with references to 'delivering' learning. We need to move away from the 'delivery' metaphor. Pizzas and babies can be delivered: learning can't. Learning is something that individual learners do. Good teaching stimulates good learning. The delivery metaphor is unsuited to the educational, social and economic needs of the future, as Davison points out: 'A delivered curriculum does not imply the need for a thinking teacher who is developing critical thinking in pupils' (Davison 2008: 31).

This book is based on some fundamental principles of, and beliefs about, teaching and learning which underpin learners' success. These principles suggest that effective learning and teaching:

- tends to be student centred rather than teacher centred;
- is based on constructivist principles;
- is active learning;
- is deep learning;
- develops learners' higher-level skills and cognition;
- develops learners' self-confidence, self-esteem and sense of 'agency';
- develops wider skills, such as problem-solving and communication, which are transferable to employment and further learning;
- helps learners to 'learn how to learn'.

Ten principles

These principles were developed from research undertaken by the Teaching and Learning Research Project (TLRP) which analysed key findings from projects in primary and secondary schools. Their findings can just as easily be applied to the lifelong learning sector.

Effective teaching and learning:

1   *Equips learners for life in its broadest sense*
    This is about developing learners as 'active citizens' who can develop their intellectual, personal and social resources. Much of learning in schools and colleges is prescribed and outcomes can be narrow. This principle requires us to look to the development of broader outcomes, such as equity and social justice.

2   *Engages with valued forms of knowledge*
    Teachers in lifelong learning should have a thorough understanding of the subjects they teach so as to engage learners with the big ideas and key processes of those subjects. However, as Coffield asks, 'whose valued forms of knowledge? The government's? The tutor's? The student's? Experts in the field?' (Coffield 2008: 12).

3   *Recognizes the importance of prior experience and learning*
    This principle is a clear link with constructivist theories of learning and also with Malcolm Knowles' theory of andogogy (Knowles 1978) which suggests that adult learners have considerable life experiences and want to have these recognized in their learning.

4   *Requires the teacher to scaffold learning*
    'Scaffolding' is an important educational concept which means that teachers can help learners by providing them with support structures to help them build their learning. These structures are gradually removed as the learning becomes secure.

5   *Needs assessment to be congruent with learning*
    There are two aspects to this. The first is that assessment should advance learning and help learners to learn; in other words, formative assessment or assessment for learning. The second aspect echoes John Biggs's concept of 'constructive alignment' in which learning outcomes and assessment objectives are matched and assessment has maximum validity.

6   *Promotes the active engagement of the learner*
    Learners should be actively involved in their learning rather than passive 'consumers' of knowledge 'delivered' to them. This principle argues for the 'active engagement' of learners and the development of independence and autonomy by increasing their repertoire of learning strategies.

7   *Fosters both individual and social processes and outcomes*
    The first aspect of this principle affirms the importance of the social aspects of learning; of people cooperating and collaborating. In constructivist theory this is also known as co-constructionism. The second aspect argues for giving learners a 'voice' and consulting them about their learning.

8   *Recognizes the significance of informal learning*
    Not all learning happens in the classroom or other educational settings. Informal learning which happens in, for example, homes and workplaces is significant and can fruitfully be linked to more formal learning. There is a link here to situated learning theory.

9   *Depends on teacher learning*
    In terms of CPD this is the most important of these ten principles. Improvements in teaching and learning are clearly related to the need for teachers to continually develop, to enhance their knowledge and skills and develop their roles, particularly through classroom inquiry and action research.
10 *Demands consistent policy frameworks with support for teaching and learning as their primary focus*
    This principle argues for consistent policy frameworks at institutional and systems level. For CPD this means that institutions and senior managers should recognize the fundamental role of teaching and learning in improving colleges and learning providers.

Effective lifelong learning and building learning power

In *Building Learning Power* Guy Claxton (2008) asserts his belief that we should be creating environments where young people (and, we suggest, people of all ages) can build their belief in themselves as learners and develop the positive attitudes and abilities necessary to become lifelong learners. To this end he proposes 'The Four R's of Learning Power' as the fundamental principles of learning and 'The Learning Power Palette' which describes the ways in which teachers can develop learning power. The following sections are taken directly from his book, which is well worth following up.

The Four R's of Learning Power

Resilience – being ready, willing and able to lock on to learning

Absorption	– flow; the pleasure of being rapt in learning
Managing distractions	– recognizing and reducing interruptions
Noticing	– really noticing what's out there
Perseverance	– 'stickability'; tolerating the feelings of learning

Resourcefulness – being ready, willing and able to learn in different ways

Questioning	– getting below the surface; playing with situations
Making links	– seeking coherence, relevance and meaning
Imagining	– using the mind's eye as a learning theatre
Reasoning	– thinking rigorously and methodically
Capitalising	– making good use of resources

Reflectiveness – being ready, willing and able to become more strategic about learning

Planning	– working learning out in advance
Revising	– monitoring and adapting along the way
Distilling	– drawing out lessons from experience
Meta-learning	– understanding learning and yourself as a learner

Reciprocity – being ready, willing and able to learn alone and from others

Interdependence – balancing self-reliance and sociability
Collaboration – the skills of learning with others
Empathy and listening – getting inside others' minds
Imitation – picking up others' habits and values

These four R's of learning power, Claxton suggests, can be promoted by the methods that teachers use and the ways in which they interact and work with their learners. The components of the 'Learning Power Palette' are:

Explaining – telling students directly and explicitly about learning power

Informing – making clear the overall purpose of the classroom
Reminding – offering ongoing reminders and prompts about learning power
Discussing – inviting students' own ideas and opinions about learning
Training – giving direct information and practice in learning

*Commentating – conveying messages about learning power through informal talk,
and formal and informal evaluation*

Nudging – drawing individual students' attention to their own learning
Replying – responding to students' comments and questions in ways
that encourage learners to learn
Evaluating – commenting on difficulties and achievements
Tracking – recording the development of students' learning power

Orchestrating – selecting activities and arranging the environment

Selecting – choosing activities that develop the four R's
Framing – clarifying the learning outcomes behind specific activities
Target-setting – helping students to monitor their own learning power targets
Arranging – making use of displays and physical arrangements to
encourage independence

Modelling – showing what it means to be an effective learner

Reacting – responding to unforeseen events, questions, etc. in ways that
model good leaning
Learning aloud – externalising the thinking, feeling and decision-making of a
learner-in-action
Demonstrating – having learning projects that are visible in the classroom
Sharing – talking about their learning careers and histories

(Claxton 2002: 69)

Continuing the theme of learning power and building learners' self-belief in their ability to learn, Claxton and Lucas (2010) consider the most recent developments in our understanding of intelligence and argue persuasively that intelligence is 'learn-able' rather than fixed. These new understandings of intelligence, they argue, can change our ways of thinking about learning and open up new possibilities for education.

Themes and topics for teaching and learning CPD

This section sets out a number of key ideas or concepts as suggested starting points for developing your CPD ideas or as a basis for action research (see Chapter 8). Each section provides an overview of the topic with suggested activities for development and opportunities for reflection. References for further reading and research are provided at the end of this chapter. These should be considered as 'starters' for investigation, not comprehensive guides.

Developing a wider range of teaching and learning techniques

An obvious CPD opportunity is to review and develop your range of teaching and learning techniques. To be an effective learner in this sector you will need a repertoire of methods to meet the needs of a diverse range of learners. Here are some suggestions you can follow up:

- case study
- discussion
- student presentations
- demonstration
- brainstorming
- buzz groups
- projects
- role play
- concept mapping
- games and quizzes discovery learning
- problem-based learning
- coaching

What might this mean for my CPD?

- Having a willingness to explore and develop new techniques.
- Taking risks in trying out new techniques and reflecting on their adaptation and development.
- Recognizing that your preferred way of learning is not necessarily the same as that of your students.
- Using peer observation and support to evaluate new techniques.

Lifelong learning

The publication of David Blunkett's *The Learning Age: A Renaissance for a New Britain* (DfEE 1998: 2) suggested an optimistic future for lifelong learning in Britain, not just for the economy and the development of skills, but also for individuals: 'learning throughout life can build human capital by encouraging, creativity, skills and imagination. The fostering of an enquiring mind and the love of learning are essential for our future success'. It has been suggested that the years since this report have seen a watering down of this vision and a concentration solely on skills, particularly those related to the needs of the economy (see, for example, Hargreaves 2004). Lifelong learning has become associated with adult learning and particularly with the needs of the economy and the skills agenda. Non-vocational and leisure courses are often seen by governments as non-productive with funding cut accordingly.

We now have a 'lifelong learning sector' – previously referred to as post-compulsory education or further education – which implies that lifelong learning is something that happens after compulsory schooling. However, lifelong learning should mean what it says, that is, 'learning lasts for life – "cradle to grave"' (Hargreaves 2004: 1). But the instrumental view of the role of the sector is still prevalent. This view is clearly endorsed by Kevin Brennan, Minister for Further Education in a letter to the *Times Educational Supplement FE Focus* headed 'Colleges at the heart of our skills-centric future' (Brennan 2009). It is undeniable that learning, particularly in the LLS, has a vital role in the development of skills and furthering the economic health of the nation. However, given that there will be many jobs in the future which don't yet exist, how do we know what skills will be required? Of David Blunkett's trio of 'creativity, skill and imagination' only skill seems to remain.

So, what can we in the LLS do to meet this 'skills-centric' vision yet still provide an education that instils a love of learning and a willingness to continue learning from the cradle to the grave? Many learners coming to the sector have not enjoyed significant success in their compulsory schooling and, consequently, have limited belief in their own capacity to learn. We need to concern ourselves not just with what people learn but how they learn and continue to learn. Guy Claxton and colleagues at the University of Bristol have identified seven general principles of learning which can serve as a basis for building learners' self-belief and autonomy. Table 6.1 outlines these principles and shows the opposite states or behaviours.

Table 6.1 Principles of lifelong learning

Principle	State or behaviour	Opposite state or behaviour
Growth orientation	The belief that learning can be learned	Stuck or static
Meaning-making	Seeking to make connections	Fragmentation Unconnected 'bits' of learning
Critical curiosity	The desire to find things out	Passivity
Resilience	Robustness and resilience in relation to learning	Dependence and fragility
Creativity	Trying out different ways	Rule bound Unadventurous
Learning relationships	Learning with others as well as on one's own	Dependence Isolation
Strategic awareness	Sensitivity to one's own learning	'Robotic'

(Adapted from Deakin Crick et al. 2004)

What might this mean for my CPD?

There are some clear messages for those teaching in this sector. It is important to:

- familiarize yourself with the history, development and key issues in lifelong learning;
- appreciate that lifelong learning implies 'learning to learn' as much as teaching subject/content;
- understand the need to encourage learners' belief in themselves as learners. This has implications for how we communicate with learners and create positive learning environments;
- understand more about how people learn most effectively;
- engage in reading and research beyond and outside of your sector. What developments are there in primary and secondary school and in universities? Are there opportunities for collaborative working, particularly as part of a Diploma partnership?
- appreciate that teachers are lifelong learners too. Part of this is your need for CPD and to develop your skills as lifelong learners.

Deep learning

In the second principle of learning shown above (Table 6.1), 'meaning-making' is crucial to effective learning. It is connected to the constructivist theory of learning and tells us that individuals make meaning from the messages they receive from the various inputs: learning cannot be 'delivered' or transmitted as if it were a package to be unwrapped. This point is eloquently discussed by Gordon Wells ('Conversation and the reinvention of knowledge' in Pollard 2002: 236) who asserts that: 'it is not possible, simply by telling, to cause students to come to have the knowledge that is in the mind of the teacher. Knowledge cannot be transmitted. It has to be constructed afresh by each individual'.

The key to helping learners create meaning is to understand how people learn. To understand deep learning we can start by comparing it to *surface learning*. Surface learning is characterized by rote learning, memory and low-level cognitive activities rather than understanding. It can only usually be reapplied in the same situation in which it was learned. While memorization is not in itself undesirable – learners may be required to memorize the periodic table or the lines of a play – real learning only occurs when the information is connected to previous learning.

The concept of deep learning was originally developed from research by Marton and Saljo (1976) who gauged groups of students' responses to reading a text. One group subsequently recalled a list of disjointed information and failed to comprehend the point the author was making. The second group set out to understand the text and what the author was trying to say. To use a building metaphor, surface learners collected 'bricks' of information with no clear idea about how to assemble the building. Deep learners built frameworks into which they could fit the bricks to make a meaningful building. However, even the best learners may struggle to make these frameworks on their own; they need teachers to provide overviews and help them to see connections. Using advance organizers (see below) can be helpful with this.

Deep learning is about really understanding a subject, making connections and recognizing underlying principles. Deep learning is most likely to be developed by student-centred activities, such as problem-based learning; reflection; case studies; application; evaluation and analysis. Deep learning is long lasting. It is associated with constructivism in that it requires the development of schema and the making of connections. Deep learning is best achieved when learners have their curiosity aroused and are set challenging problems.

As with learning styles, we need to be careful not to label learners simplistically as 'surface learners' or 'deep learners'; things are rarely this simple. Some learners will be surface in some situations; deep in others. Some learners will take a 'strategic' approach which has the characteristics of surface learning but is actively chosen by learners who are not intrinsically interested in that topic but need to have some understanding of it.

What might this mean for my CPD?

- Engaging in further research into deep and surface learning.
- Do you use teaching and learning methods which are likely to encourage deep learning?
- Sharing the concepts of deep and surface learning with your learners. This kind of 'metacognitive' activity helps learners to reflect on and improve their own learning.

Advance organizers

To help learners build the bricks of knowledge into a building, teachers can help by providing advance organizers to give them an idea of what the finished building should look like. To use a different metaphor, advance organizers can help learners to 'map the territory' of the new region of learning they have entered into.

Advance organizers are devices for providing organizational frameworks which teachers present to learners to prepare them for what they are about to learn. They link previous knowledge and learning to the coming topic or provide the 'big picture' for new learning. As well as preparing for learning to come, organizers can be used for revising learning; connecting learning and discovering new ideas and concepts; analysing and thinking. Examples of advanced organizers include:

- concept maps
- flow charts
- diagrams
- written overviews
- charts
- timelines
- maps
- tree diagrams

- bullet points
- series of steps

What these organizers do most effectively is to 'fix' an idea or concept so that new learning can be related to it. In English literature, a teacher can fix the structure and characters in a play or novel by a visual representation. Organization charts help business studies students see the structures of businesses clearly and analyse and evaluate them. Advanced organizers which use a visual element are sometimes called 'graphic organizers'. Thinking visually can help learners and teachers to become more familiar with the big concepts in a subject and with structuring ideas and solving problems. Dan Roam in his book *The Back of the Napkin* shows how initial thoughts and ideas can be captured and developed using a range of visual techniques (Roam 2008). Similarly, concept mapping provides opportunities for teachers and learners to produce the big picture and explore connections. Tony Buzan has developed the concept of 'mind mapping' and offers a range of publications and services to support it. There are several concept mapping tools available which you can buy, or sometimes download for free on your computer; MindGenius is a good example.

Sometimes an advance organizer can consist simply of a concise spoken, or written, introduction to a session which sets out the key issues to be considered or questions to be answered. Margaret Archer, writing about educational systems, begins her article with an admirably simple overview: 'How do educational systems develop and change? This first question about the characteristics of education can be broken down into three subsidiary ones: "Who gets it?"; "What happens to them during it?" and "Where do they go after it"?' (Archer in Pollard 2002: 363). Immediately we know where we're going and what the main issues are.

What might this mean for my CPD?

- Use a search engine to find a range of sites offering 'graphic organizers'. Use or adapt some of the ideas you find.
- Develop advance organizers to help learners understand a block of learning or even a whole course. A course diagram or map can help learners to see the big picture of the course and the elements within it. Course maps and diagrams can be included in student handbooks and made up as posters.
- Introduce your learners to advance organizers, concepts maps and visual thinking and encourage them to use them, especially in small group work.

Formative assessment

Formative assessment is an integral part of the teaching and learning process and its aim is to promote learning and to motivate learners; it is assessment *for* learning. Summative assessment – assessment of learning – is the summing up or checking of learning at particular stages by, for example, testing or some kind of formal assessment.

Some of the most significant work on formative assessment has been carried out by Black and William (1998); the influence of their work is evident in the Qualification and Curriculum Authority's (QCA) guidelines on Assessment for Learning (QCA 2001). Black and William provide some basic premises to support the use of formative assessment, which are worth quoting in full. Their work is the result of research in schools but the conclusions are equally valid for learners of all ages, particularly adult returners who have basic skills needs; consequently, we have substituted the word 'learner' for 'pupil' in the following:

> the research indicates that improving learning through assessment depends on five, deceptively simple, key factors:
>
> - the provision of effective feedback to [learners];
> - the active involvement of [learners] in their own learning;
> - adjusting teaching to take account of the results of assessment;
> - a recognition of the profound influence assessment has on the motivation and self-esteem of [learners], both of which are crucial influences on learning;
> - the need for [learners] to be able assess themselves and understand how to improve;
>
> At the same time, several inhibiting factors were identified. Among these are:
>
> - a tendency for teachers to assess the quantity of work and presentation rather than the quality of learning;
> - greater attention given to marking and grading, much of it tending to lower the self-esteem of [learners], rather than to providing advice for improvement;
> - teachers not knowing enough about their [learners'] needs.
>
> (Black and William 1998: 17)

What might this mean for my CPD?

- Review your assessment formats and procedures. Do you provide assessments that are designed to improve and develop learning or are they mainly about summative assessment and grading?
- Are the purposes and requirements of assessments clear to learners? Do they know why they are doing them?
- Do you provide effective and developmental feedback to learners to help them improve and develop?
- Assessment doesn't have to be formal. It can be informal, such as the use of questioning and discussion.

Employability

It could be argued that employability has always been at the centre of education but is more explicitly referred to in current educational discourse. The debate concerning education for the economy versus education of the 'whole person' is not new. I would argue, however, that this is a false division. The most important elements of success in work and life are the kinds of learning experiences that people have and their belief in themselves as learners. The attitudes, abilities and skills of being a good learner are the same as those of a good employee or, indeed, self-employed person. Many young business people report that, for them, the old distinctions between work, life and learning are blurred.

Sir Andrew Foster's (2005) report made clear recommendations regarding the purpose of further education: 'perhaps our most crucial recommendation is that colleges should sharpen their focus and direct the main force of their effort towards improving employability and supplying economically valuable skills' (p. 3). The political focus has, for some time now, been shifting towards the development of employment skills in education, particularly since the Leitch Report in 2006. One of the difficulties is what is meant by 'employability skills'; as Martin et al. suggest: 'Definitions of employability skills range from a vague notion of having something to do with preparing for a first job, through to very precise lists of specific skills, and on to employability being seen as a learning process' (Martin et al. 2008: 7).

What do employers want?

When asked what skills and qualities they want in new, young employees, employers suggest a range of generic skills in addition to job-specific skills. These employer 'wish-lists' usually include:

- communication skills
- team-working skills
- problem-solving skills
- literacy skills
- numeracy skills
- general IT skills
- timekeeping
- business awareness
- customer care skills
- personal presentation
- enthusiasm/commitment
- enterprise.

There is a temptation to deliver employability as a series of self-contained, 'bolt-on' activities in short courses and workshops. However, it may be more realistic and effective to consider ways in which employability can be developed within an integrated curriculum. The key to this is to offer a broad range of learning activities which encourage deep learning, thinking skills and problem-solving. Employability is best considered as a learning process.

What might this mean for my CPD?

- Developing employability is a responsibility for all teachers in the lifelong learning sector.

- Do you consider a range of teaching and learning activities which will develop not only employability, but also deep learning and thinking?
- Integrated projects, particularly work-related ones, can motivate learners and develop their employability. Projects can bring together a wide range of learning opportunities, including for example: communication; problem-solving; ICT; presentation; and evaluation.
- Have you worked with careers, information, advice and guidance staff in your institution to develop work-related projects?
- For your students on work experience or those in work-based learning, do you make links between theory and practice; between what they do in the classroom and what they do in the workplace?

Thinking skills

Thinking skills are centred on deliberate, purposeful, structured thinking processes which are learned and developed through application and practice. When we talk about thinking skills we are usually referring to a range of higher order thinking processes. Fisher (2006: 25) suggests that: 'Such processes include remembering; questioning; forming concepts; planning; reasoning; imagining; solving problems; making decisions and judgements; translating thoughts into words and so on.' McGuiness (1999) says that thinking skills include:

- collecting information
- sorting and analysing information
- drawing conclusions from information
- 'brainstorming' new ideas
- problem-solving
- determining cause and effect
- evaluating options
- planning and setting goals
- monitoring progress
- decision-making
- reflecting on one's own progress.

Personal, learning and thinking skills (PLTS)

Diploma learning combines theoretical and applied learning together with Functional Skills and personal, learning and thinking skills. The latter are set out in a framework (see QCDA website below). The six skills will require learners to become:

- independent enquirers
- creative thinkers
- reflective learners
- team workers

- self-managers
- effective participators.

In common with other facets of learning such as problem-solving and employability, thinking skills are best developed using an 'embedded' approach rather than a discrete approach. This requires teachers to broaden the range of teaching and learning techniques to develop higher-order thinking and learning. The links and further reading below contain many useful ideas for you to follow up. One of the keys to developing thinking skills is to share the ideas behind it with your own learners and get them to reflect on their own learning and thinking; metacognitive activities such as these are vital in producing independent learners.

What might this mean for my CPD?

- Read and research into thinking skills and ways in which you can embed them.
- Encourage your learners to consider and reflect on their thinking and how they learn. The use of learning logs and discussion can be very useful for this.
- Develop a range of teaching and learning techniques which include thinking skills.

Problem-based learning

Most learning begins with learning something particular (knowledge and skills) and then, hopefully, using it to solve problems. Problem-based learning (PBL) works the other way round; it begins with the problem and asks learners to identify what knowledge and skills they already have but also what additional learning they need in order to solve the problem.

Problem-based learning began in medical and health education as a response to the situation in which some health professionals had a wealth of knowledge but fewer problem-solving skills. If you think about it, turning up at the doctor's or at the hospital with a complaint is about asking a health professional to make a diagnosis and solve your medical problem. Similarly, turning up at a garage with a spluttering, underperforming car is about asking a motor vehicle technician to solve your car's problem. Much of our working lives is concerned with solving problems; it doesn't take too much thought to extend the above examples to include business; engineering; science; design; construction; health and social care; and social work training.

Problem-based learning, as far as I am aware, has not been widely used in post-compulsory education and lifelong learning. In FE colleges, in particular, teachers feel that they do not have sufficient course time to indulge in PBL and similar strategies. This is a real concern, but sometimes it's necessary to take risks. John Biggs states that PBL 'is not so much a method as a total approach to teaching, which could embody several possible TLAs [teaching/learning activities] and assessment methods' (Biggs and Tang 2007: 151). In this respect, PBL provides an ideal integrating focus on the Business and Technology Education Council (BTEC), the new Specialized Diplomas and similar vocational courses, but might be less viable for A level students.

The kind of PBL practised in universities might be too large scale for use in lifelong learning but we can use the principle and adapt it to some smaller scale activities. Let's consider a few possible problems:

- with a car
- with behavioural difficulties in children
- in IT or electrical equipment
- of accessibility and mobility in a building
- with the profitably of a company (this might have begun life as a case study)

What might this mean for my CPD?

- Research the theory and methods of problem-based learning.
- Work with colleagues, and learners, to identify meaningful problems as a basis for learning.
- Identify problems which are not only relevant to the curriculum but also to the lives and experiences of the learners.

Personalized learning

Personalization and personalized learning are likely to become an increasingly important element in education at all levels. It could be argued that far from another educational 'fashion' it is a more realistic view of how people learn. In the future it might be considered odd that 20 or more people were put in a room and a teacher 'delivered' a standard input to them all and expected them all to make roughly the same progress in the same amount of time. People spend only a small part of their lives learning in this way.

> Personalisation aims to make *every* student's learning experience responsive to his or her particular interests. It invites teachers to involve their learners in decision-making and to plan for their learning to maximise their motivation, relate to their background, draw on their strengths and take account of their preferred learning styles.
>
> (LSIS)

The Department for Education and Skills issued a consultation document in 2006, *Personalising Further Education: Developing a Vision* (DfES 2006b), which sets out its plans to introduce 'a range of changes to strengthen personalisation in FE and make a reality of the 14–19 Skills Strategies'. In summary, personalization is defined thus: 'In an educational setting, personalisation means working in partnership with the learner and employer – to tailor their learning experience and pathways, according to their needs and personal objectives – in a way which delivers success' (DfES 2006: 7).

The development and use of initial and diagnostic testing and ILPs provides a firm foundation for the introduction of personalized learning, but this is only part of the picture. To be successful personalization needs a 'total curriculum' approach and should include consideration of the following elements:

- understanding learning and how people learn
- extending the range of teaching and learning strategies
- creating a 'thinking' curriculum
- learning to learn
- assessment for learning
- personal learning plans
- harnessing technology to support personalization
- listening to and building on the student voice.

Building from personalization is the concept of the 'expert learner'. This concept brings together a number of key elements by which teachers and learners working together can develop expert learning. These elements include: independent learning; listening to the learners' voice; learning how to learn; and assessment for learning. The Gold Dust resources for teacher educators, hosted by LSIS, provides further resources to support this initiative (see below).

Behaviour management

The development of the 14–19 agenda and widening participation policies have resulted in a more diverse range of learners in the LLS. Many teachers in the sector have reported behaviour management as one of their key concerns in relation to these new cohorts. While their concerns are undoubtedly genuine, some research suggests that younger learners feel better treated in colleges than they do in school.

One of the respondents in Harkin's research into the Increased Flexibility Programme (IFP) stated: 'School teachers tell you off for nothing and just tell you to do something . . . they should be more like college teachers: let you do things in your own way; give you a choice of what you want to do' (Harkin 2006: 325).

One of the first things you might want to investigate is the extent to which there is a shared definition of 'bad behaviour' among you and your colleagues. The same group of learners might be an 'awkward squad' to one teacher but a lively and bustling group to another.

Activity

- List the kinds of behaviour you consider to be 'bad'.
- What is it about these behaviours that makes them 'bad'?
- If you have done this as a group, is there a consensus about the definition of 'bad' behaviour? What different perceptions are there?

What might this mean for my CPD?

- Carrying out further research into behaviour and motivation.
- Engaging discussion and research with colleagues and sharing of good practice.
- Researching causes of behaviour problems; individual; psychological; family; society.
- Are learners different in different situations? Some learners who are restless and difficult in formal teaching can be well behaved and motivated in more practical learning.
- Are there practical strategies to ameliorate behaviour problems? You might want to consider planning and structure of sessions; communication style; content; teaching and learning methods; resources.

Using technology

Mark Prensky (2001) uses the concepts of 'digital natives' to describe those young enough to have grown up with ICT and 'digital immigrants' to refer to those who have had to learn it all in later life. It seems clear that young people are very adept at using a range of new technologies and constantly adapting to developments and customizing to suit their needs. The picture is not as clear, however, when it comes to adult learning, particularly those in low income groups. Research evidence suggests that information technologies in education have, to some extent, tended to reinforce existing inequalities in access and achievement. It has been stated that:

> [T]he evidence is strong that, despite many efforts to use technology to overcome social exclusion, it has tended to reinforce social divisions, with people who use the internet for learning, or for gathering information, tending to be those with the highest levels of previous education, and the best access to traditional learning.
>
> (McNair and Quintero-Re 2008: 82)

Becta carries out considerable work in supporting the research and development of ICT in education. In a recent document (Becta 2009a: 4) it outlines some of the ways in which technology is changing colleges but suggests that, 'if technology is changing the way colleges operate, it is still having too little impact on the role of the teacher'. According to Becta, colleges are currently spending up to 80 percent of their information technology (IT) budgets just on keeping their systems running, leaving little for innovation. This problem is exacerbated by young people coming to college whose domestic IT equipment is, most likely, more advanced than the college can provide; and an ageing workforce, some of whom will not be up to speed in using technology. To support colleges in their ICT development Becta offers a range of services including the 'Generator Technology Improvement Tool'. To promote a more positive attitude to ICT Becta suggest that teachers need ongoing support and training 'without fear of judgement. Training and development should be about raising confidence and enabling staff'

(Becta 2009a: 8). Moreover, ICT developments are not simply related to technology but also to a new, more learner-centred understanding of learning and teaching in which teaching is more about creating a learning environment than transmitting facts.

Using PowerPoint

PowerPoint is a useful tool, but don't let it become the only tool in your box. Like other resources, it's there to support teaching and learning not to dictate the form and structure of it. Your first step in planning a session should not be the production of a PowerPoint presentation. So what's wrong with this technology? Basically, nothing; it's how it is used that's the problem. In one of the first critiques of PowerPoint, Edward Tufte (2006: 13, original emphasis) claims that: 'The core ideas of teaching – *explanation, reasoning, finding things out, questioning, content, evidence, credible authority not patronizing authoritarianism* – are contrary to the cognitive style of PowerPoint.' Tufte goes as far as to assert that 'bullet outlines can make us stupid'. The main criticism is that PowerPoint encourages, almost compels, teachers to adopt a linear structure. Such linear structures, organized around bulleted lists and stock PowerPoint templates with, frequently annoying or irrelevant, Clipart, can all too easily reinforce teacher-dominated sessions with learners as mere 'viewers' probably not even bothering to take notes because they know they will be given a printout of the slides. Teachers in the LLS are becoming more familiar with constructivist learning theory and the importance of finding ways to help learners construct and critique their own learning. A useful method to support this is the concept map, a device which doesn't feature on PowerPoint templates. Constructivist learning and teaching and concept maps show learners that knowledge and ideas exist in complex and changing networks, not in the simple linear steps chosen by the teacher. So should we abandon PowerPoint completely? No, but we should start to use it more creatively and reject the easy options provided by stock templates. Try to avoid bullet points. Don't let style become more important than content. Try to use it non-sequentially so that you don't have to plough tediously through a set sequence. A good way is to make your first slide a mind map with each bubble linked by an action button to a slide further up the sequence or different presentation altogether. Make hyperlinks to documents in your memory stick and to websites.

What might this mean for my CPD?

- Research new technology applications. For example, have you used wikis or blogs? Could you use them?
- Are you worried that your learners might know more about using technology than you do? They almost certainly will, but this can be an opportunity for you to learn from them and to encourage them to reinforce and develop their skills by transferring them to other contexts.
- Do you prepare a PowerPoint presentation for every session? If so, why? Have you considered using PowerPoint more creatively?
- Can you competently include hyperlinks, action buttons and/or audio and video clips in your presentations?
- What training courses are available, in-house or externally, to support your ICT development?

- Have you considered working with colleagues, and perhaps students, to develop your skills and knowledge collaboratively?
- Are you encouraging your learners to push their ICT learning and to apply it in other contexts, even if you don't fully understand them?

Further reading and sources of information

Brain-based learning and neuroscience

Geake, J.G. (2009) *The Brain at School: Educational Neuroscience in the Classroom.* Maidenhead: Open University Press.

OECD (2002) *Understanding the Brain: Towards a New Learning Science.* Available free online from: www.dcsf.gov.uk/research/data/uploadfiles/DCSF-RW030.pdf

The results of a massive research project by the OECD's Centre for Educational Research and Innovation (CERI).

Developing teaching and learning

Eastwood, L., Coates, J., Dixon, L. et al. (2009) *A Toolkit for Creative Teaching in Post-compulsory Education.* Maidenhead: Open University Press.

Scales, P. (2008) *Teaching in the Lifelong Learning Sector.* Maidenhead: Open University Press. Chapter 5 'Teaching and learning methods'.

Websites

LSIS Gold Dust Resources for teacher educators. A comprehensive website with a wide variety of resources developed by teachers and teacher educators. http://golddust.bdplearning.com/index.php

TeacherNet http://www.teachernet.gov.uk/teachingandlearning/

Lifelong learning

Deakin Crick, R., Broadfoot, P. and Claxton, G. (2004) 'Developing an effective lifelong learning inventory: the ELLI project'. *Assessment in Education: Principles, Policy and Practice,* 11(3): 247–72.

Hargreaves, D. (2004) *Learning for Life: The Foundations of Lifelong Learning.* Bristol: Policy Press.

Rogers, J. (2009) *Adults Learning,* 5th edn. Maidenhead: Open University Press.

Schuller, T. and Watson, D. (2009) *Learning Through Life: Inquiry into the Future of Lifelong Learning.* Leicester: National Institute of Adult Continuing Education (NIACE).

Websites

NIACE (The National Institute for Adult Continuing Education). http://www.niace.org.uk/

Research and development; campaigning and publishing on a wide variety of topics and issues in adult education.

The Centre for Research on the Wider Benefits of Learning. www.learningbenefits. net
>   Based at the Institute of Education, University of London. Provides a wide variety of reports on the wider, particularly social and well-being, benefits of learning.

Deep learning

Biggs, J. and Tang, C. (2007) *Teaching for Quality Learning at University.* Maidenhead: Open University Press.

Websites

James Atherton's Learning and Teaching site. Article on deep and surface learning: Atherton, J.S. (2009) *Learning and Teaching; Deep and Surface learning* (online). Available: http://www.learningandteaching.info/learning/deepsurf.htm (accessed 15 November 2009).

James Atherton thoughtfully supplies a critique of deep and surface learning: Atherton, J.S. (2008) *Doceo: For Surface Learning* (online). Available: http://www.doceo.co.uk/heterodoxy/surface.htm (accessed 15 November 2009).

Advance organizers

Buzan, T. and Buzan, B. (2006) *The Mind Map Book (Mindset).* London: BBC Active.

Harris, I. and Caviglioli, O. (2003) *Think it – Map it.* Stafford: Network Educational Press Ltd.

Novak, J.D. (2009) *Learning, Creating and Using Knowledge: Concept Maps as Facilitative Tools,* 2nd edn. London: Routledge.

Roam, D. (2008) *The Back of the Napkin: Solving problems and selling ideas with pictures.* London: Portfolio: The Penguin Group Ltd.

Websites

British Council/BBC *Teaching English* http://www.teachingenglish.org.uk/think/articles/graphic-organisers

Eduplace – graphic organizers http://www.eduplace.com/graphicorganizer/

Freemind Free mindmapping software http://freemind.software.informer.com/

MindGenius mind-mapping software www.MindGenius.com

Formative assessment

Jones, C.A. (2009) *Assessment for Learning.* London: Learning and Skills Improvement Service.

Tummons, J. (2005) *Assessing Learning in Further Education.* Exeter: Learning Matters.

Websites

LSIS Gold Dust resources for teacher educators. *Assessment for Learning*: http://golddust.bdplearning.com/assessment_for_learning/index.php

Employability

Frier, H. and White, P. (2006) *Key Skills and Employability Through Work-related Learning and Enterprise*. London: Learning and Skills Development Agency.

Gravells, A. (2010) *Delivering Employability Skills in the Lifelong Learning Sector*. Exeter: Learning Matters.

Hind, D. and Moss, S. (2005) *Employability Skills*. Sunderland: Business Education.

Martin, R., Villeneuve-Smith, F., Marshall, L. and McKenzie, E. (2008) *Employability Skills Explored*. London: Learning and Skills Network.

Websites

Connexions Jobs4u has a useful 'jobs families' section and case studies: http://www.connexions-direct.com/jobs4u/

The Vocational Learning Support Programme offers 'The Recruitment Game: materials to support student success after school'. This site also has a comprehensive list of additional sources of information about generic employability skills: http://www.excellencegateway.org.uk/VLSP29/index.htm

Thinking skills

Bowkett, S. (2006) *100 Ideas for Teaching Thinking Skills*. London: Continuum. An accessible book with lots of ideas for developing thinking skills.

Caviglioli, O., Harris, I. and Tindall, B. (2002) *Thinking Skills and Eye Q*. Stafford: Network Educational Press Ltd.

Costa, A. (ed.) (2001) *Developing Minds: A Resource Book for Teaching Thinking Skills*. Alexandria, VA: Association for Supervision and Curriculum Development. A real 'treasure house' of a book with contributions from a wide range of experts.

de Bono, E. (1985) *Six Thinking Hats*. London: Penguin Books.

Fisher, R. (2003) *Teaching Thinking*, 2nd edn. London: Continuum. Although written for primary teachers it's well worth a look whatever sector you teach in.

Key Skills Support Net (2008) *Getting Ahead with Personal, Learning and Thinking Skills: Lessons from the Wider Key Skills*. London: Learning and Skills Network. Downloadable from www.keyskillssupport.net

McGregor, D. (2007) *Developing Thinking; Developing Learning: A Guide to Thinking Skills in Education*. Maidenhead: Open University Press.

Websites

http://www.teachingthinking.net/ Robert Fisher's website on teaching thinking and creativity

www.philosophersnet.com 'The Philosopher's Magazine' has a section on 'café philosophique' and some interesting and amusing debates, a recent example, 'Shakespeare vs. Britney' considers questions of what art is.

Problem-based learning

Weyers, M. (2006) *Teaching the FE Curriculum*. London: Continuum.
Problem-based learning has developed mainly in universities but Chapter 8 of this book provides a good introduction to its use in FE.

Websites

Atherton, J.S. (2009) *Learning and Teaching: Problem-based Learning* (online). Available: http://www.learningandteaching.info/teaching/pbl.htm (accessed 29 October 2009). This website is comprehensive and always worth a look for trainee and experienced teachers.
http://www.bized.co.uk/current/pbl/educator.htm Provides resources for Business education. The *Problem Based Learning: Guide for Educators* is a useful resource.

Personalized learning

DfES (Department for Education and Skills) (2006) *Personalising Further Education: Developing a Vision*. London: DfES.
TLRP (Teaching and Learning Research Programme) (n.d.) *Personalised Learning: A Commentary by the Teaching and Learning Research Programme*. London: Economic and Social Research Council.

Websites

LSIS Excellence Gateway http://www.excellencegateway.org.uk/page.aspx?o=131209 Contains useful background information and advice, plus case studies and links to other websites such as Becta.
LSIS Excellence Gateway *Developing the Expert Learner* http://tlp.excellencegateway.org.uk/tlp/xcurricula/el/gettingstarted/overview/index.html
LSIS Gold Dust resources for teacher educators. *The Expert learner*: http://golddust.bdplearning.com/planning_for_learning/the_expert_learner.php
Develops the concept of the 'expert learner' and links it to personalization. Very useful range of resources for teacher educators.
The Diploma Support website is a comprehensive collection of documents and support programmes for those involved in Diploma teaching. It is equally useful for all involved in the lifelong learning sector.
http://www.diploma-support.org/resourcesandtools/handbooks Personalised Learning handbook

Behaviour management

Rogers, B. (2007) *Behaviour Management: A Whole-school Approach*. London: Paul Chapman.

Scales, P. (2008) *Teaching in the Lifelong Learning Sector*. Maidenhead: Open University Press (Chapter 9 'Motivation and behaviour').

Vizard, D. (2007) *How to Mange Behaviour in Further Education*. London: Paul Chapman Educational Publishing.

Websites

Behaviour4learning Positive Approaches to Behaviour Management http://www.behaviour4learning.ac.uk/

www.behavioursloutions.com. Dave Vizard's site provides support and training in behaviour management for schools and colleges.

Using technology

Becta (2008) *Harnessing Technology: Next Generation Learning 2008–14. A Summary*. Coventry: Becta. All the above available from www.becta.org.uk/publications

Beetham, H. and Sharpe, R. (2007) *Rethinking Pedagogy for a Digital Age*. London: Routledge.

Clarke, A. (2006) *Teaching Adults ICT Skills*. Exeter: Learning Matters.

Hill, C. (2008) *Teaching with E-learning in the Lifelong Learning Sector*. Exeter: Learning Matters.

LLUK (2009) *Application Guides: Using Technology to Support Learning for Teachers, Tutors and Trainers in the Lifelong Learning Sector*. London: LLUK. This application guide makes specific links between the LLUK Professional Standards and the effective use of technology.

LLUK (2009) *Using Technology to Support Learning for Teachers, Tutors, and Trainers in the Lifelong Learning Sector*. London: LLUK.

This document is based on the LLUK professional standards. For each standard advice and applications are suggested. Illustrative case studies are also available.

Richardson, W. (2006) *Blogs, Wikis and Podcasts and Other Powerful Web Tools for Classrooms*. Thousand Oaks, CA: Corwin Press.

Websites

JISC http://www.jisc.ac.uk Support and information on a variety of learning technology projects.

Learning Technologies – Learning and Skills Network www.learningtechnologies.ac.uk

MoLenet The main site of the Mobile Learning Technologies project http://www.molenet.org.uk/

Prezi.com presentation software http://prezi.com/ This offers some interesting and enjoyable opportunities for breaking out of PowerPoint's linear style.

7 Subject-specific CPD

Our very best teachers are those who have a real passion and enthusiasm for the subject they teach. They are also deeply committed to the learning of their students and use their enthusiasm for their subject to motivate them, to bring their subject alive and make learning an exciting, vivid and enjoyable experience.

(DfES 2003: 1)

This chapter is about:

- Mapping the territory of your subject specialism
- Auditing your own subject knowledge and skills
- Ideas for subject specialist CPD activities
- Subject specialist mentoring
- 'Selling' your subject
- Helping learners find their way into your subject
- A subject specialist directory
- Resources for subject specialist CPD

Even the briefest glance at a college prospectus, an adult and community learning programme or the services offered by training providers makes us aware of the wide variety of learning and training offered, from A level physics to beginners French; from Foundation Degree engineering to Foundation Learning Tier programmes. Unlike most initial teacher training for schools, which is subject-based, training for the LLS is usually general in nature. Subject-specific mentors have been part of the training for teachers in this sector for a long time, even before the changed programmes – P/C/DTLLS – introduced in 2007. However, the availability and quality of subject mentors couldn't always be assured. Ofsted's survey (2003) of initial teacher training in FE reported that:

It is assumed that trainees will already have the necessary specialist skills, or that they will receive specialist training within the college faculties or departments in which they work. While this may be true in some cases, many new FE teachers do not receive this specialist input. In some highly specialised curriculum areas, there may be no one else with the relevant expertise within the college on which the new teacher can draw.

(Ofsted 2003: 23)

The new training programmes, however, make the necessity of subject specialist development and mentoring explicit. This is underpinned by the LLUK Professional Standards Domain C which sets out the standards for professional values, knowledge, understanding and practice relating to specialist learning and teaching. The four key values of Domain C are shown below to provide a context for this chapter and some starting points for considering your subject-specific CPD.

Teachers in the lifelong learning sector are committed to:

CS1   Understanding and keeping up to date with current knowledge in respect of own specialist area

CS2   Enthusing and motivating learners in own specialist area

CS3   Fulfilling the statutory responsibilities associated with own specialist area of teaching

CS4   Developing good practice in teaching own specialist area

Your specialist subject – mapping the territory

What do you teach? How well do you know your subject? Many teachers come into the sector, particularly in colleges, as highly trained and knowledgeable experts in their subjects, teaching, for example psychology or engineering. Equally, there are those who will have begun their teaching careers in a particular subject area but choose, or are required, to become teachers of related subjects; for example, an English teacher who turns her hand to media studies or a literacy specialist who also develops as a numeracy specialist. Fisher and Webb (2006: 342) refer to the tendency of vocational curricula in FE colleges to 'atomize', providing the example of a business studies department traditionally used to running business studies or economics courses which is required to prepare trainees for the workplace through E2E (Entry to Employment) courses or new 'bundles of knowledge and skills', such as 'managing people' or 'business communication'. These kinds of provision are often part of the college's need to maintain a competitive advantage, particularly in the context of increasing numbers of training providers.

Opportunities to extend the range of your teaching can be exciting and refreshing and are vital elements in a lifelong learning organization but teachers who do this need support, training and continuing professional development as part of an agreed professional development plan. Stepping outside of your subject specialism is also important for how we understand and organize knowledge and relate different areas of the curriculum to each other. Subjects are in many ways artificial constructs, whose boundaries are clearly marked, but in reality they overlap and merge. It is more challenging and interesting for you and your learners if you can make links between your own specialist area and others and to your learners' interests. These kinds of inter-subject connections encourage the development of thinking skills and remind us that in the 'real world' knowledge and skills are not compartmentalized in such rigid ways.

Part of our work with learners is to help them be successful in the current stage of their learning but also to help them progress to the next stage or to a related area of work or study. Subject specialists should know the progression routes and the levels at which their subject is available. Teachers working with students on Foundation Learning Tier programmes, for example, need to be able to provide information, advice and guidance for their learners' progression.

This section uses the term 'mapping the territory' as a metaphor to help you think about your own subject specialism and your familiarity with the extent and the detail of it. Even if you don't teach some of the more distant areas of your specialist terrain, it's good to know about it so that you can see where your 'bit' fits in and what parts your colleagues teach. The paradox of being a specialist is that we can become too 'specialist'. I have encountered university lecturers who are experts in their specialism but deliver modules with little or no knowledge of the other elements of the programme. If teachers can't see the big picture and make connections, their learners won't be able to.

The following activity gives you an opportunity to map the territory of your subject. To get a more complete picture this is probably best done as a team exercise. The activity will also be useful if you are considering changes to the course or shifting to another assessment board and, more importantly, for planning subject-specific CPD.

Activity

This activity is to help you map the territory of your subject specialism. It's important to not just think about the particular examining body specifications you work to or the content and methods of the subject where you currently work.

This might at first appear to be an exercise in the obvious, but sometimes it's useful to explain things to ourselves in order to understand them more fully.

1   What precisely do you teach? Is it a single subject, such as biology, or is it a wider general area such as health and social care?
2   Is it a 'subject' or a 'bundle of knowledge and skills' (Fisher and Webb 2006: 342)? If the latter, what are the constituents of this 'bundle'?
3   Can you produce a map or visual representation of your specialism?
4   Is there a clearly defined syllabus or specifications for your subject or can you define or negotiate the content?
5   Have you compared with other specifications?
6   How easy is it to define and explain your subject to a non-specialist?
7   What are the main areas of your specialism?
8   What are the most recent developments in your subject specialism?
9   What levels of study are available within your subject specialism? What are the progression routes open to learners in that specialism?

Auditing your own subject knowledge and skills

Having mapped the territory of your subject specialism a useful next step in planning CPD is to audit your own, and your team's, skills and knowledge. The knowledge and skills gaps between what the course specifications require and what you know and can do provide some fruitful possibilities for CPD.

You should be thorough in your auditing and aim to get a complete picture of your knowledge, skills, experience and abilities. Some elements will be obvious, such as educational qualifications or work experience; others may be less obvious but equally valuable, such as experience gained from voluntary or community work, or from a leisure activity. This kind of activity is a useful 'stock-take' and gives you an opportunity to review your CV.

Activity

Carry out an audit of your own subject knowledge, skills and experience. You will find the following headings useful but will want to add others of your own.

- Formal educational qualifications from Level 2, or equivalent qualifications, to your highest level of qualification. If any of your qualifications have transcripts of what you learned, include these;
- Other qualifications as part of your work;
- Any other training undertaken as part of your work;
- Remember that to be a teacher in the LLS, you must have a Level 2 qualification in literacy and numeracy;
- Previous work experience. Think carefully about all the elements of your job/s. What precisely was your job? What were the main elements of it?
- Have you developed relevant skills and knowledge from your leisure interests?
- Are you a member of a professional body? Are you required to provide evidence of CPD for this body?

Models of continuing professional development

As discussed in Chapter 1, 'old-style' CPD frequently consisted of staff development courses which people were required to attend. This kind of 'sheep-dip' approach to CPD is becoming outmoded and we are, albeit gradually, moving towards a more personalized approach in which teachers are at the centre of the process and are able to decide what is needed for improving teaching and learning and for the success of their students. It is important that teachers seize this opportunity and recognize it as part of being a professional.

It is useful to consider the range of CPD activities in terms of the extent to which they have the potential to put the teacher at the centre and to develop professional autonomy. Kennedy (2005) proposes nine models of continuing professional development and provides a critical discussion of them within a framework which builds from those involving 'transmission' to those which are 'transformative'. While recognizing that those which are transformative and build teacher autonomy are most likely to bring deep changes, it is acknowledged that 'transmission' models are sometimes necessary, particularly in the introduction of new ideas and methods.

1   *The training model* In this model CPD is generally 'delivered' to teachers by experts who determine the scope and content of the training. This view of CPD can be criticized as being essentially 'transmitting' information from experts to passive novices although it can also be an effective means of introducing new knowledge.

2   *The award-bearing model* This is similar to the above model but results in some form of accreditation or award from an external body, such as a university, which has credibility in terms of quality assurance. Again, this has the benefit of providing an effective introduction to new areas but the temptation for managers is to rely too heavily on these models because they provide easily auditable evidence of training and development.

3   *The deficit model* This model begins with the notion of a 'deficit' in individual teachers which needs to be met in order to meet standards or rectify a weakness. While it might occasionally be the case that teachers do have a deficit and would appreciate some training to bring them up to speed, CPD based on this model tends to be demotivating and can lead to a 'blame the teacher' mentality. Continuing professional development is best undertaken in an ethos of 'appreciative inquiry' or 'appreciative coaching' (see Chapter 1).

4   *The cascade model* This kind of development is often based on an understandable desire to save money by one, or a few, teachers attending an event and disseminating the information to colleagues. This may, depending on the content of the original event, be an efficient way to share new information and ideas but it overlooks the possibility that the context, the participation and collaboration of that event can't necessarily be replicated in any meaningful sense.

5   *The standards-based model* This is, essentially, training and development having the primary purpose of meeting standards, for example LLUK standards. In common with competence-based training, standards-based training can be criticized for its tendency to reduce teaching to a common, standardized, set of values, behaviour, knowledge and practice while belittling the notion of individual teacher 'artistry'. However, as Kennedy (2005: 242) points out, "Arguably, standards also provide a common language, making it easier for teachers to engage in dialogue about their professional practice."

6   *The coaching-mentoring model* This model is explained by its title. Increasingly mentoring is seen, particularly in the LLS, as one of the most effective means of CPD, particularly for new entrants to the profession. An effective one-to-one relationship is at the heart of this model. The more effective this relationship is, the more likely it will be that the learning process is

transformative. A mentor who is a poor communicator or one who has been co-opted into the role will, at best, merely transmit information.

7 *The community of practice model* This model is based on the work of Wenger (1998) who suggests that we are all members of communities of practice in various settings. There are, according to Wenger (1998: 95) three essential processes in a community of practice:

- evolving forms of mutual engagement
- understanding and [tuning] their enterprise
- developing [their] repertoire, styles and discourses

The most beneficial aspect of a successful community of practice is that new learning and development results from the interaction of its members rather than from pre-planned objectives or outcomes prescribed prior to the activity of the group.

8 *The action research model* Action research is based within a particular setting, for example, learning and teaching, and involves the practitioners in that setting improving the quality of action within it. It can be most effective when carried out within a community of practice. This kind of CPD activity is at the top of the scale for transformation of practice and encourages teacher autonomy by recognizing their central role in understanding and improving their practice, rather than having things 'done to them' by experts (see Chapter 8).

9 *The transformative model* Kennedy suggests that this, in itself, is not a model, rather it is 'the combination of practices and conditions that support a transformative process' (2005: 246). In this view of CPD a 'transmission' activity, such as an input from a visiting expert, can be part of a transformative process if it informs teachers and, subsequently, gives them the opportunity to apply, evaluate and experiment with it and use it to generate new ideas and practices.

The main reason for discussing these models is to give you some ideas about how you can evaluate your CPD activities in terms of the extent to which they transform your teaching and students' learning. In cash-strapped environments even the best management teams will want to find the most effective and efficient methods of CPD. However, teachers need to be proactive in persuading managers and budget-holders that the easiest is not always the best. If we really want to improve teaching and learning and put it at the heart of what we do, we need to invest time and money in transformative CPD activities.

Subject-specific CPD activities

This section is intended to provide you with some general ideas for activities for subject-specific CPD activities. This is just a sample of some of the most usual activities, however, it is important that you consider the full range of possibilities within your specialism because there may be things you do as a matter of course which you don't consider to be CPD. For instance, for a trainee teacher of film and media studies who needs to teach French New Wave cinema watching films is perfectly acceptable as CPD.

In its review of CPD 2008–9, the IfL makes the point that CPD based on professional dialogue about teaching and learning is the most effective. It goes on to say that: 'There is an over-focus on formal courses. Personalised CPD, such as peer coaching, is underdeveloped, yet research shows that this is the most effective' (IfL 2009c: 11). References and website addresses are provided at the end of this chapter.

Gaining qualifications

You might want to update your knowledge and skills by gaining a specific qualification in your subject area or to develop your range of expertise by studying for a qualification in a related discipline. If you are a subject specialist in, for example, a vocational area you could investigate a Foundation Degree. These are designed in conjunction with industry and employers to address skills gaps and to upskill the workforce. They include a wide variety of specialisms, for example, manufacturing management; sport studies; early years and childhood practice; multi-media design. Foundation Degrees are equivalent to the first two years of an honours degree and you will have the opportunity to top up to a full degree.

You might also want to consider gaining a qualification in Skills for Life (literacy, numeracy or English for speakers of other languages – ESOL) as a Skills for Life specialist or as a vocational teacher who wants to work more effectively with Skills for Life specialists. You will, of course, need to be up to date with Functional Skills, especially in relation to the new Diplomas.

Once you have begun studying, from PTLLS upwards, FE colleges and universities will be keen to offer a range of higher courses through first degree, masters and doctorate.

Industrial updating

One of the strengths of further education has always been the experience that vocational staff bring with them from their previous work in business and industry. It is important for all learning providers to develop links with industry through placements, secondments and work shadowing.

To facilitate such activity LLUK and Skills for Business have developed the Catalyst programme which aims to increase links between education, training and business. One of their services, Business Interchange, encourages the development of work experience placements for teachers and trainers.

Examiner, verifier and assessor roles

Undertaking assessor and verifier roles provides excellent opportunities to develop both elements of dual professionalism and give you the opportunity to see student work within your place of work or, as an external verifier, in other colleges and training providers. External work offers great opportunities for networking and sharing ideas. Further information on assessor and verifier awards is available on the main awarding body websites.

Working with awarding bodies

The main awarding bodies offer a wide range of support, from downloadable documents to bespoke training programmes. You should check out the services available from the awarding body for your course; don't leave it to the course leader. If you are new teacher it is especially useful to look at the subject specifications, past examination papers and examiners' reports. Awarding bodies provide training events, particularly when there are changes to courses or new specifications are introduced. It is often the case that colleges and learning providers will send one representative to meetings and ask that person to 'cascade' the information – another excellent CPD opportunity.

Giving presentations

Giving presentations to colleagues at work or in the wider setting of a conference provides excellent opportunities for developing both sides of the dual professional. As mentioned above, you may be reporting back on a training session you have attended or you may be organizing and running a staff development activity. As well as giving you an opportunity to research and develop your subject expertise, these events also challenge you to hone your presentation skills. The IfL points out that 'the least frequent activities engaged in were research and contributions to journals and conferences' (IfL 2009c: 11).

Writing

There are always opportunities for writing for a range of purposes and audiences, whether as printed documents or as online writing. These opportunities may be report writing to inform or persuade colleagues, or writing articles for specialist journals or for more general publications, such as the IfL's *InTution* journal. Many specialist bodies and networks encourage and accept book reviews and articles from specialists; websites increasingly provide blogging opportunities. If you and your colleagues are involved in an action research project, you will need to write up the results and disseminate to colleagues and the wider subject community.

Even if you don't consider yourself to be a writer, if you've got something to say, it's likely that other people will want to hear it. Just write, then get someone to help you with structure, grammar, spelling and the technical aspects.

Reading

Reading books, articles, reports and websites is a 'taken for granted' activity, but is frequently a legitimate and justifiable CPD activity. If you're teaching English Literature obviously you will need to read the set texts, but you can also benefit from reading other relevant books – history, sociology – to provide context. Specialists who are members of professional bodies will receive publications and journals which contain valuable advice, links and networking opportunities. Academic and specialist journals are easily available online now and colleges will have subscriptions and electronic access to organizations such as the British Educational Index, Educational Resources Information Centre (ERIC) and the EBSCO electronic journals service. Libraries can be a bit intimidating for the uninitiated – just go in and ask, the staff will want to help.

The above activities are just a few suggestions for subject-specific CPD. The IfL CPD guidelines provide further examples which you might want to follow up.

Sector Skills Councils (SSCs)

Sector Skills Councils are employer-led organizations representing specific economic sectors in the United Kingdom. They are licensed by the government through the UK Commission for Employment and Skills (UKCES). They were set up to achieve four specific goals:

- to reduce skills gaps and shortages;
- to improve productivity;
- to boost the skills of the sector workforces;
- to improve the learning supply.

At present there are 25 SSCs involved in the development of national occupational standards (NOSS) and designing apprenticeship frameworks. Sector Skills Councils are a valuable resource, especially if you are involved in the new Diplomas. On each SSC website you will find a range of information relating to occupational standards, training, resources, careers and professional bodies. It's also a good way to keep up to date with the goals and key developments within each sector.

All of the current SSCs and their web addresses are listed in Table 7.1. There will be one for your subject area.

Specialist Schools and Academies Trust (SSAT)

Specialist schools status has now been applied to over 3 000 secondary schools in England. The SSAT is an independent, not-for-profit membership organization with over 5600 schools and organizations, which works with headteachers, teachers and students to raise standards across the secondary educational system. The SSAT also works to promote collaboration between schools and colleges, in particular through the diploma lines with a view to enabling positive links between subject specialisms in schools and colleges and to further develop good practice in curriculum and pedagogy.

The SSAT has a variety of personalized CPD programmes to support specialist practitioners, including the provision of lead practitioners who will undertake CPD

Table 7.1   UK Sector Skills Councils (SSCs)

Sector Skills Council	Sector	Website
Assett Skills	Property; housing; cleaning and facilities management	www.assettskills.org
Cogent	Chemicals; pharmaceuticals; nuclear; oil and gas; petroleum and polymers	www.cogent-ssc.com
Construction Skills	The construction sector and the development and management of the built environment	www.ccskills.org
Creative and Cultural Skills	Advertising; crafts; music; performing; heritage; design and the arts	www.ccskills.org.uk
e-skills UK	Business and information technology	www.e-skills.com
Energy and Utility Skills	Electricity and renewables; gas; waste management and water industries	www.euskills.co.uk
Financial Services Skills Council	Financial services; accountancy and finance	www.ffsc.org.uk
GoSkills	Passenger transport	www.goskills.org
Government Skills	Skills for central government	www.government-skills. gov.uk
Improve	Food and drinks manufacturing and processing	www.improveltd.co.uk
Lantra	Environmental and land-based sector	www.lantra.co.uk
Lifelong Learning UK	Community learning; education; FE; HE; libraries; work-based learning and training providers	www.lluk.org
People 1st	Hospitality; leisure; travel and tourism	www.people1st.co.uk
Proskills UK	Process and manufacturing sector	www.proskills.co.uk
SEMTA	Science, engineering and manufacturing technologies	www.semta.org.uk
Skillfast-uk	Fashion and textiles	www.skillfast-uk.org
Skills for Care and Development	Social Care; children and young people	www.skillsforcareand development.org.uk
Skills for Health	Represents the whole of the UK health sector	www.skillsforhealth.org.uk
Skills for Justice	Fire and rescue services; policing and law enforcement; youth justice; custodial care; community justice; courts service; prosecution service and forensic science	www.skillsforjustice.com
Skills for Logistics	The logistics sector	www.skillsforlogistics.org
SkillsActive	Active leisure and learning	www.skillsactive.com
Skillset	Audio visual industries	www.skillset.org
Skillsmart Retail	Retail sector	www.skillsmartretail.com
SummitSkills	Building services engineering	www.summitskills.org.uk
The Institute of the Motor Industry	Retail motor industry	www.motor.org.uk

with schools to improve knowledge in both subject and pedagogical approaches and to develop subject networks. Those working in the LLS should look particularly at the '14–19' and 'specialism' pages on their website.

Subject-specific mentoring

Mentoring, especially subject-specific mentoring, is increasingly being seen in the LLS as one of the most effective forms of CPD and personal development. Much has been published on mentoring and coaching; this section provides a brief introduction and signposts to more detailed sources are given at the end of the chapter.

Mentoring and coaching are frequently discussed as if they were interchangeable. MacLennan (1995) makes a simple distinction between a coach, someone you learn *with*, and a mentor, someone you learn *from*. Whereas coaching can be seen more as a way to help someone grow and help them to discover their talents and improve performance, mentoring is more concerned with learning from a more experienced practitioner. Pollard (1997: 19) defines mentoring as, 'The provision of support for the learning of one person through the guidance of another person, who is more skilled, knowledgeable and experienced in relation to the context of the learning taking place'.

The role of the mentor and mentoring skills

Wallace and Gravells (2005: 4) provide a comprehensive discussion of the role and importance of the mentor, particularly the subject-specific mentor supporting trainee teachers. They identify the key responsibilities of a mentor as:

- to model good classroom practice;
- to contribute to the assessment of the student teacher's classroom practice;
- to *support* the student teacher's grasp of subject knowledge in terms of currency, breadth and appropriate structure for presentation to learners;
- to *assess* the student teacher's grasp of subject knowledge in terms of currency, breadth and appropriate structure for presentation to learners.

In past industrial times a new recruit to a job often learned by 'sitting next to Nellie' and observing her skills and methods. This model worked well if Nellie was keen to pass on her skills and support new recruits. If, however, Nellie was an embittered and cynical worker and an unwilling teacher, her services would be less than useful. In a modern environment, a good and effective mentor needs to have or develop a variety of skills to support their mentees, including:

- planning
- liaising
- demonstrating

- facilitating
- observing
- assessing
- guiding
- questioning
- listening
- reflecting.

Effective mentoring requires patience and empathy. You may recall learning a new skill and feeling uncertain of your suitability to do it and being unable to assess your progress. A patient mentor guides and supports the mentee as they learn, as well as showing empathy for the new practitioner and remembering what it was like for themselves when they started.

Subject learning coaches (SLCs)

The SLC programme is part of the Teaching and Learning Programme which you can access through the LSIS website. The role of the SLC is to act as a change agent within a particular subject specialism in an organization to develop subject strategies, resources and best practice; to provide individual and group training and to use peer coaching techniques to support the improvement of teaching and learning. The SLC programme is built around three interconnected 'enablers': teaching and learning resources; subject coaching networks; and the professional training programme.

Teaching and learning resources

The 'Gold Dust' resources which have been available in physical form and were distributed to all learning providers are now available online. They provide a wide range of materials to support the development of teaching and learning (for example, using questions; developing active learning) in subject settings. The subject resources library includes:

- business
- construction and built environment
- creative and media
- engineering
- foundation learning
- IT
- land-based
- mathematics
- science
- society, health and development
- modern foreign languages

Subject coaching networks

Subject coaching networks are one-day regional events which take place at least twice a year. At these sessions participants can experiment with the teaching and learning resources and try out new approaches to teaching and learning in their subject area. In addition they provide networking opportunities and chances to practise coaching skills with peers. Currently, the subject networks are:

- adult learning
- business education
- creative and media
- construction and the built environment
- E2E (foundation learning)
- society, health and development
- IT
- land-based studies
- modern foreign languages

The LSIS STEM programme provides support and resources for science, technology, engineering and mathematics.

Professional training programme

Professional training is provided through the ALC training programme. While SLCs work with colleagues at subject and team level to improve teaching and learning the ALC programme is more strategic in focus and aims to develop participants to work with senior managers to develop organizational CPD and quality improvement plans.

'Selling' your subject

We are often called upon to 'sell' our subjects to prospective students, and their parents, at open days and marketing events. On a wider level we may sometimes find that we have to justify our subjects to senior management who are feeling the financial pinch and want to cut courses, and to governments who might not see the 'usefulness' of them. We are all familiar, for example, with the debates around Media Studies, which is frequently unfairly targeted as being 'easy' or having no real career possibilities.

Education, particularly in the LLS, is increasingly expected to provide answers to a range of problems including employability; skills for the economy; tackling social exclusion; and education for sustainability and the environment. In construction and the built environment, for example, awarding bodies and curriculum have had to include knowledge and skills relating to energy conservation. A useful exercise can be to argue the benefits of your subject specialism and to 'sell' it to a range of audiences. The following activity takes as its starting point two standards from the LLUK:

CK 1.2 Ways in which own specialism relates to the wider social, economic and environmental context

CP 1.2 Provide opportunities for learners to understand how the specialist area relates to the wider social, economic and environmental context

---

Activity

Your task is to 'sell' your subject to four separate audiences

1   Learners
2   Employers and business
3   People concerned about the environment and sustainability
4   People wanting to develop social inclusion and community

Step 1
Begin by considering the possible objections from these audiences. Why might they not want to buy this educational 'product'?

How would you counter these objections?

Step 2
Brainstorm the positive selling points of your subject. What can it offer that will directly or indirectly benefit the four audiences?

This activity can be a way of motivating your students and helping them to see the relevance of the subject. It also offers possibilities of making links with, for example, businesses and community organizations.

From a teaching and learning perspective the activity provides opportunities for group work; research; visits; presentations; making displays; making videos; wikis and blogs.

Helping your learners to find their way into your subject

One of the most important tasks for a teacher is to invite learners into their subject, not only to become familiar with the content and skills but also to help them to understand it a deep level and develop ways to think and talk about it. Some teachers are very welcoming; others less so. This is not just a matter of the teacher's personality or style, it's something we can all develop. If you recall learning in any subject or discipline at any stage of your life, but particularly within an educational institution, you will remember that you didn't know everything at once. Some elements – a few key concepts; some key words – might have been familiar to you, but the big picture will have been indistinct and potentially alienating. You will also, no doubt, recall gradual realization and piecing together of a more complete understanding. Teachers can help learners to do this; we can help them find 'ways in'.

The idea of 'finding a way in' brings together both sides of the dual professionalism model – subject specialism and teaching and learning. We have already considered some of the pedagogical elements in Chapter 6, particularly the use of advance organizers to help learners understand the 'big picture' and constructivist learning theory which emphasizes the role of previous learning and the development of personal understandings and schemas.

Relevance

Students will find it easier to get into a subject if they can see its relevance. How does it relate to real life? How does it relate to their previous experience and can teachers help them to make connections? Learners often feel that they are thrown in at the deep end of a subject rather than splashing about in the shallow end and gradually developing the confidence to move up. In some areas of learning, for example, maths, science and engineering, teachers may have been used to filling learners up with content prior to applying and analysing it. Kember et al. (2008: 254), writing of first year teaching at university suggest that:

> It was not just that the abstract theory aroused little interest, it was also hard to understand in many cases. Without seeing an application which put the theory in context it became hard to grasp the meaning. It was also difficult to frame suitable questions to advance understanding.

If students' first experiences of a subject are seemingly unconnected bits of theory and unusual terminology, they are likely to feel confused and demotivated. Supplying reasons and contexts for learning from the outset will increase motivation. Relevance can be established by, for example:

- using real-life examples
- drawing cases from current issues
- giving local examples
- relating theory to practice.

In subjects such as sociology and health and social care, new students will probably know about a range of social issues but will be unfamiliar with the concepts and language the subject specialism uses to understand and discuss these things. Northedge (2003a; 2003b) gives an example of how we can begin with the familiar and use it as a way into the subject and its discourse. The first step is to capture students' attention and establish a common focus for understanding and meaning-making. He illustrates this by an example from social work training in which students are introduced to and discuss a case study of two homeless drug users. By this everyday, 'common-sense' discussion students can relate to a real-life scenario and start to tease out some of the key issues. The discussion would not necessarily include subject-specific language and concepts. The second step leads from familiar to specialist discourse by discussion and questioning and the introduction of specialist concepts. A further advantage of this process, implicit in Northedge's work, is that students can develop their critical thinking skills as they move from 'common-sense' understandings and opinions to more rigorous and objective, academic understandings. Northedge's ideas seem to challenge conventional wisdom that students need to acquire theory/content before they can apply it to problems. Sometimes introducing problems first can be a stimulating introduction and increase motivation to develop the understanding of theory.

Threshold concepts

A recent development in learning theory is the idea of 'threshold concepts'. These are particularly associated with the work of Meyer and Land (2003; see also Land et al. 2008) who suggest that 'threshold concepts may be a way of overcoming the "stuffed curriculum"'. They refer to 'A tendency among academic teachers . . . to stuff their curriculum with content, burdening themselves with the task of transmitting vast amounts of knowledge bulk and their students of absorbing and reproducing this bulk' (p. 26). This may be true of vocational teachers as well as academic. Focusing on 'threshold concepts' can help to teachers to identify what is fundamental to students' grasp of the subject.

Three of the key features of threshold concepts are that they are:

- transformative – they make a difference to who we are and how we perceive the world. They change our ways of understanding.
- irreversible – once understood they are unlikely to be forgotten. Teachers can find it difficult to recall a time when they didn't understand these concepts and, therefore, find it difficult to empathize with students who are struggling with them.
- integrative – they help students to make connections. As Cousin (2006: 4) points out, 'mastery of a threshold concept often allows a learner to make connections that were hitherto hidden from view'. There is a clear link here to constructivist theories of learning.

'Socialization' is an example of a threshold concept from sociology. Initially difficult for students to grasp, once mastered it provides a basis for understanding much of sociology. It is transformative, irreversible and integrative.

Stokes et al. (2007: 436) provide examples of threshold concepts in other disciplines:

Economics	– opportunity cost; elasticity
Pure Mathematics	– complex numbers; limits
Electrical Engineering	– frequency response
Statistics	– sampling distribution
Computer Science	– object oriented programming
Law	– precedence

Table 7.2 TDA list of subject associations (adapted)

Subject	Association	Website
All subjects	Subject Association	www.subjectassociation.org.uk
Art & Design	National Association for Education in Art and Design (NSEAD)	www.nsead.org
Biology	Institute of Biology	www.iob.org
Business and economics	Economics and Business Education Association	www.ebea.org.uk
Chemistry	Royal Society of Chemistry	www.rsc.org/education
Citizenship	Association of Citizenship Teaching	www.teachingcitizenship.org.uk
Classics	Joint Association of Classical Teachers	www.jact.org
Dance	National Dance Teachers Association (NDTA)	www.ndta.org.uk
	The Royal Academy of Dance	www.rad.org.uk
Design technology	Design and Technology Association	www.data.org.uk
	National Association of Advisers and Inspectors in Design and Technology	www.naidt.org.uk
Drama	National Drama	www.nationaldrama.co.uk
English	National Association for the Teaching of English	www.nate.org.uk
	The English Association	www.le.ac.uk/engassoc
	National Association of Advisers in English	www.naae.org.uk
	The Poetry Society	www.poetrysociety.org.uk
English as an additional language	National Association for Language Development in the Curriculum	www.naldic.org.uk
Geography	Royal Geographic Society	www.rgs.org
	Geographical Association	www.geography.org.uk
History	Historical Association	www.history.org.uk
	Schools History Project	www.tsc.ac.uk/shp/
ICT	The Association for Information Technology in Teacher Education (ITTE)	www.itte.org.uk
Literacy	United Kingdom Literacy Association	www.ukla.org
	National Association of Writers in English	www.nawe.co.uk
Mathematics	Advisory Committee on Mathematics Education	www.royalsoc.ac.uk/acme
	National Centre for Excellence in the Teaching of Mathematics (NCETM)	www.ncetm.org.uk
	The Mathematical Association (MA)	www.m-a.org.uk
	Association of Teachers in Mathematics	www.atm.org.uk

(continued)

Table 7.2 TDA list of subject associations (adapted) (*continued*)

Subject	Association	Website
	Institute of Mathematics and its Applications (IMA)	www.ima.org.uk
	National Association for Numeracy and Mathematics in Colleges (NANAMIC)	www.nanamic.org.uk
Media	Media Education Association	www.mediaedassociation.org.uk
Modern languages	CILT The National Centre for Languages	www.cilt.org.uk
	Association for Language Learning	www.all-languages.org.uk
Music	National Association of Music Educators (NAME)	www.name2.org.uk
	Music Education Council	www.mec.org.uk
Physical education	Association for Physical Education	www.afpe.org.uk
Physics	Institute of Physics	www.iop.org
Religious education	The RE Council for England and Wales	www.religiouseducationcouncil.org
	The National Association of Teachers of Religious Education (NATRE)	www.natre.org.uk
Statistics	Royal Statistical Society	www.rss.org.uk
Science	Association for Science Education	www.ase.org.uk
	Science, Engineering and Technology Board (SCENTA)	www.scenta.co.uk

http://www.tda.gov.uk/teachers/ continuingprofessionaldevelopment/curriculumsubjects.aspx

---

Activity

Can you identify any 'threshold concepts in your subject specialism?

For example, in sociology and media studies, 'ideology' can be a really difficult concept to grasp. Equally, using concepts such as 'horsepower' or 'torque' in motor vehicle courses can be challenging.

In what ways can you help your learners to understand these concepts? Don't be frightened of 'dumbing down'; use a picture, a diagram or a model.

Another feature of threshold concepts, as defined by Meyer and Land (2003) is that they involve 'troublesome knowledge'. Knowledge is 'troublesome' in the sense that while individuals are coming to grips with this new knowledge it may seem alienating, counter-intuitive, or just plain scary. Once the learner has passed through this threshold state of partial understanding, they may feel transformed; if they get stuck they may only partially understand the concept and, consequently, encounter barriers to further understanding in the subject. It's worth taking time and effort to ensure that learners fully understand these threshold concepts.

A subject specialist directory

The TDA provide a list of subject specialist associations which teachers in the LSS might also find useful. This list is based on formal associations. There are many other sites for whatever subjects you teach; a good start is simply to type 'subject resources' plus your specialism into a search engine (see Table 7.2).

Further reading and sources of information

Foundation degrees

www.fdf.ac.uk

Skills for Life and Functional Skills

LSIS Excellence Gateway http://excellence.qia.org.uk
The Skills for Life Network www.skilsforlifenetwork.com
The Skills for Life National Reference Point http://www.lluk.org/skills-for-life.htm
QCDA Functional Skills provides standards; training; resources and support for Functional Skills http://www.qcda.gov.uk/22100.aspx
DCSF 14–19 Reform Functional Skills http://www.dcsf.gov.uk/14-19/index.cfm?sid=3&pid=225&ctype=None&ptype=Contents

The Catalyst Programme

This programme is aimed at extended the experience of teachers through industrial placements and encouraging experienced professionals into teaching. www.catalystprogramme.org
The Business Interchange is concerned specifically with arranging work placements. http://www.catalystprogramme.org/business-interchange

Examiner, verifier and assessor roles

City and Guilds http://www.cityandguilds.com/9554.html?search_term=7317
Edexcel http://www.edexcel.com/quals/nvq/ass-ver/Pages/default.aspx

Specialist Schools and Academies Trust

Particularly the sections on '14–19' and 'Specialism' https://www.ssatrust.org.uk/Pages/home.aspx

The Teaching and Learning Programme

This is a service of the LSIS. The home page is at: http://tlp.excellencegateway.org.uk/ teachingandlearning/downloads/index_lsis.html

The Teaching and Learning contains the following links to elements of the overall programme: Teaching and learning resources http://www.subjectlearningcoach.net/ resources2/index.aspx

'Gold Dust' resources http://golddust.bdplearning.com/

Professional Training Programme

    Training to become an Advanced Learning Coach (ALC): http://www. subjectlearningcoach.net/about_subject_learning_coaches/three_enablers/ professional_training_programme.aspx

The LSIS STEM (science, technology, engineering and mathematics) programme: http:// tlp.excellencegateway.org.uk/tlp/stem/index.php

Cross-curricular themes, including customer care and developing the expert learner: http://tlp.excellencegateway.org.uk/tlp/xcurricula/index.html

Subject coaching networks: http://www.subjectlearningcoach.net/about_subject_ learning_coaches/three_enablers/subject_coaching_networks.aspx

Training for 14–19 Diploma teaching

Harkin, J. (2007) *Excellence in Supporting Applied Learning*. A Report for LLUK and the TDA. Oxford: Westminster Institute of Education, Oxford Brookes University. http://www.lluk.org/documents/Excellence_in_Supporting_Applied_Learning.pdf

Training and Development Guidance for Teachers of Diplomas. February 2007.

Developed from the above report. http://www.lluk.org/documents/Training_and_ Development_Guidance.pdf

The report and guidance led to: Accredited Professional Development Units for 14–19 practitioners http://www.lluk.org/3482.htm

TDA Subject associations and resources

http://www.tda.gov.uk/teachers/continuingprofessionaldevelopment/ curriculumsubjects.aspx

8 The teacher as researcher

Research is a high-hat word that scares a lot of people. It needn't. It's rather simple. Essentially, research is nothing but a state of mind . . . a friendly, welcoming attitude toward change . . . going out to look for change instead of waiting for it to come. Research is an effort to do things better and not to be caught asleep at the switch. It is the problem-solving mind as contrasted with the let-well-enough-alone mind. It is the tomorrow mind instead of the yesterday mind.

(Charles Kettering 1958–1976, quoted in Hubbard and Power 2003)

This chapter is about:

- Definition and characteristics of action research
- The action research process
- A brief review of research methodology
- Ethics in research
- Benefits and limitations of action research
- Case studies of action research

Teachers teach; researchers research. For many teachers in the LLS this simple proposition remains true and the notion of themselves as researchers seems alien; something arcane and complex that academics do to produce conclusions and propositions which may, or may not, filter down to teachers. Teachers are frequently the subjects of research; less frequently the initiators of it. The concept of the teacher as researcher has been around for some time. In 1975 Lawrence Stenhouse suggested, 'It is not enough that teachers' work should be studied; they need to study it themselves' (Stenhouse 1975: 143).

Action research is a very effective method for improving all elements of your practice – teaching, learning and assessment, and curriculum. It is an important aspect of any teacher's role and can be instrumental in helping colleges and learning providers make informed decisions about educational policy, practice and programmes. In addition to this the teaching profession should be committed to enabling their learners to have a full and complete knowledge of their subject and in order to achieve this staff should engage in both subject- and subject pedagogy-based research.

As teachers in the post-compulsory environment we are constantly involved in classroom instruction, through the learning and teaching methods we choose to employ; assessment and grading, whether it be formative or summative assessment; the evaluation of student performance, again either formatively or summatively, and the reflection upon our own practice. All of these activities take place while we work within the curriculum and look for ways of improving the curriculum offering. In effect what we are doing on a daily basis, often without realizing it, is undertaking research through questioning ourselves about our own teaching and our students' learning and then adapting or changing our practice to improve. We are 'teachers as learners'. If we undertake this learning in a more deliberate, rigorous and methodical manner and apply and evaluate the results in our own practice, we are also 'teachers as researchers'.

Most importantly, action research plays a key role in 'maximising the professionalism of tutors' (Coffield 2008: 21). Support for action research at organizational and national level reinforces the professionalism of teachers and helps reassure them that their understandings of their own learners and their own subjects are paramount. Action research and reflective practice are the most valuable methods for improving practice in specific contexts and, as such, are preferable to the importation of 'best practice' from other, unfamiliar, contexts.

What is research?

Chambers Dictionary defines research as 'a careful search; investigation; systematic investigation towards increasing the sum of knowledge'. The key word here is 'systematic'. Stenhouse, cited in Rudduck and Hopkins (1985: 19) defines research as 'systematic and sustained enquiry, planned and self critical'.

McNiff (1993: 5) presents two views of educational research. The first, dominant, view, is that knowledge about education is created by researchers and imposed on teachers. The research remains the 'property' of the researchers. In the second view, research is instigated and conducted by teachers within the context of their own practice. In this view teachers 'own' the knowledge resulting from the research. For McNiff, this is a process of 'teaching as learning'; it is a logical extension of reflective practice and CPD. We should note, however, that the role of conventional research is still important insofar as it provides a bank of theory and propositions which can be used to inform action researchers and to be tested in practice.

What is action research?

> Action research is a form of enquiry that enables practitioners everywhere to investigate and evaluate their work. They ask, "What am I doing? What do I need to improve? How do I improve it?" Their accounts of practice show how they are trying to improve their own learning and influence the learning of others.
>
> (McNiff and Whitehead 2006: 7)

Action research investigates practice with a view to improving the quality of a particular context or event, in this case, teaching and learning. It is normally associated with a 'hands on' approach and it can be undertaken by individuals or by teams of colleagues who work together to undertake collaborative inquiry. In short it can identify

Table 8.1 Characteristics of action research

Characteristic	Definition
Practical	Deals with real life problems
Change	Provides a solution to the problem
Cyclical	Includes an evaluation of the solution with a view to further research
Participation	Active not passive

(Adapted from Denscombe 2007: 123)

and establish a need or concern and develop methods to meet that need or make improvements to a process. Denscombe (2007) suggests that there are four defining characteristics of action research as shown in Table 8.1.

These characteristics show important distinctions between action research and conventional research, particularly in its cyclical nature and as an active process. Teachers are not just 'consumers' of research carried out by others; they are actively recognizing problems to be solved and applying and refining the results in their own context. However, when the research activity is finished the work of improvement is not complete. It is part of a continuous cycle of research, experimentation and improvement in which participants continue to review, evaluate and improve teaching and learning.

Activity

Consider the following quote from Brenda Dyck:

> When you teach a lesson and half the class gives you a blank look, you ask yourself, 'How else can I teach this concept?' That's research. You observe and respond to what you have observed. You begin to be aware of the intricate teaching and learning dance with your children. The more I tune in, the better I become at knowing when to lead, when to follow, or when to play a sedate waltz or a lively rap.
>
> (Dyck 2009)

- Reflect on the last time you experienced something like this, what did you do?
- How did you change things and what was the outcome of those changes?

Action research – an opportunity to involve your learners

Ruddock believes that 'pupils and teachers should work together to create classroom change' (Ruddock and McIntyre 2007: 2). Dialogue with, and seeking information from, learners is an important element of action research, especially with post-compulsory and adult learners. Learners may want to discuss their experiences in different sessions or in different subjects and explain what they find 'engaging, stimulating, bewildering, difficult or off-putting' (Rudduck and McIntyre 2007: 7). Teachers may find it useful to discuss teaching and learning methods with learners to evaluate and further develop them. Learners are, or should be, the main focus of any educational institution and, as such, are well placed to discuss their experiences of teaching and learning with teacher-researchers. Some of the most recent developments in teaching and learning are around the notions of more active, student-centred learning, enquiry and thinking skills. In this spirit it seems appropriate to involve learners in research or, at least, to seek their opinions and to gather data from them.

MacLean and Mohr (1999: viii) believe that their experiences as teacher-researchers have redefined and enhanced their roles as teachers. The following activity is based on a quote from their work.

Activity

> Teachers are subjective insiders involved in classroom instruction. Traditional educational researchers who develop questions and design studies around those questions and conduct research within the schools are considered objective outside observers of classroom interaction. But when teachers become teacher-researchers, the 'traditional descriptions of both teachers and researchers change. Teacher-researchers raise questions about what they think and observe about their teaching and their students' learning. They collect student work in order to evaluate performance, but they also see student work as data to analyze in order to examine the teaching and learning that produced it'.
>
> (McLean and Mohr 1999:27)

Consider your teaching role:

- What information could you collect from your learners that would help you evaluate your effectiveness in the classroom?
- In what other ways could you involve your learners in your research?
- What might be the benefits for your learners of their involvement in the project?
- What difficulties might there be in involving learners?

The action research process

The action research process at its simplest level could be described as:

- reflect upon and assess own practice
- explore and test out new methods
- evaluate the outcomes.

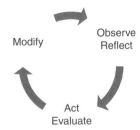

Figure 8.1 The action research cycle

This simple model, however, omits modification and continuing evaluation and research. Jean McNiff provides a more comprehensive description of the steps of the action research process, which can constitute an action plan:

- we review our current practice,
- identify an aspect that we want to investigate,
- imagine a way forward,
- try it out, and
- take stock of what happens.
- we modify what we are doing in the light of what we have found, and continue working in this new way (try another option if the new way of working is not right),
- monitor what we do,
- review and evaluate the modified action,
- and so on ...

The key point is that action research is a cyclical process as demonstrated in Figure 8.1.

So how can this be achieved in the classroom? As a teacher or practitioner undertaking research your main aim should be to improve learning and teaching practice, whether it be your own or that of your learners. The following pointers may help you in undertaking an action research project:

- collect and analyse data from classes including observations of class reaction and achievement;
- reflect upon practice and personal assumptions and beliefs;
- determine questions to be answered or problems to be solved;
- identify activities or actions that would allow you to respond to questions or create solutions;
- complete activities;
- review findings following activity completion;
- evaluate the outcome of your chosen activity;
- disseminate the results of your research. You could give presentations to colleagues or at conferences; write about your research in newsletters and

journals; run workshops and CPD sessions, or participate in teacher research websites, online forums, and email communications;
- start the process again.

A working example of action research

As part of your annual monitoring report, you have identified an area for development as being the further strengthening of subject specialist subject for the learners on programme. As a team you need to address this. You decide upon the following plan of action:

- introduce subject specialism screening at interview;
- introduce a specific ILP (Individual learning plan) for each student to assess their subject knowledge;
- create a timetable of 'milestones' that students need to achieve within their subject;
- create a subject network, making use of peer groups and learning communities.

Following the implementation of this plan of action, you evaluate the outcomes through individual case studies of impact **evaluation**.

Research methodology – a brief review

Research and finding out about how to research can be daunting activities. Researchers tend to use their own specialist terminology, some might even consider it 'jargon'. One of your first tasks as a novice researcher is to familiarize yourself with some basic concepts and to tackle some of the terminology.

Research takes place within a wide variety of settings. At a very simple level we can distinguish between scientific research such as might be undertaken in biology, chemistry or physics, and social science research such as that in education or sociology. There are three main approaches to research:

- Quantitative – tends to involve statistical data
- Qualitative – tends to involve people's perceptions of the world
- Mixed methods – a combination of the two.

Qualitative approaches to research tend to involve researchers collecting facts and data, often numerical data and studying the relationships between one set of facts and another and producing statistical generalizations. This approach is most usually associated with research in science. In social sciences, researchers are generally more concerned with people rather than things and, consequently, may take a qualitative approach and seek to discover insights and people's perceptions of the world. We should be wary of the simplistic idea that science is always quantitative while social science is always qual-itative. Some social sciences, particularly psychology, have strong scientific and math-ematical traditions. In many cases researchers will opt for a mix of the two approaches.

Regardless of the method all research will start with a research question, for ex-ample – What am I trying to achieve? Why am I doing this? How will it improve my practice? Following this the actual design of the research should be considered. Your answers to questions such as – Who will I consult? What methods of collecting in-formation are most appropriate for my question? When and how will I collect the information? – will determine the methods you will use within your action research project. Each of the approaches – quantitative, qualitative or mixed – will then have a variety of data collection methods that you could use to answer your original ques-tion: questionnaires, focus groups, interviews and observation to name but a few. This chapter does not explore research tools in any great depth as there are numerous re-search textbooks on the market that you could use to get you started. (At the end of the chapter there is a list of further reading and sources of information that you may find useful.)

Ethics in action research

Any researcher must consider the ethical issues of their research before beginning their study. All researchers should aim for the principle of 'informed consent' in relation to the subjects of their research and the uses to which it is put. This requires care and sensitivity in preparing, researching and reporting. Many of the ethical considerations surrounding action research focus on several main issues: confidentiality, privacy, con-sent, consequence, harm, and in the case of education, the power relationship between the teacher and the student. Blaxter et al. (2001: 158) provide a useful summary of the key elements of ethical practice in research:

> Research ethics is about being clear about the nature of the agreement you have entered into with your research subjects or contacts. This is why contracts can be a useful device. Ethical research involves getting the informed consent of those you are going to interview, question, observe or take materials from. It involves reaching agreements about the use of this data, and how its analysis will be reported and disseminated. And it is about keeping to such agreements once they have been reached.

Even in small-scale research, you must gain the informed consent of the respondents. You can provide a brief oral statement before interviews or other face-to-face settings explaining why you are doing this research; how it will be carried out and how it will be used or disseminated. A written version of this statement should be provided in postal questionnaires. In both cases you must reassure the respondents that their participation is confidential and will be made anonymous and explain that names will not be used in transcripts and recordings will be destroyed once they have been transcribed.

There are various ethical codes that attempt to set out the fundamental principles surrounding research in any given professional setting. The code most likely to apply to educational settings using action research would be that of the British Educational Research Association (BERA). Useful further reading on ethical issues can be found in Bell (2005) and Cohen et al. (2007).

Activity

Consider an issue that is currently affecting your work and/or workplace.

- What could be the objective of any proposed study?
- What research questions are you seeking to answer?
- What type of research approach (qualititative/quantitative/mixed methods) would be best suited to answer your questions?
- What research methods would be most appropriate to collect data?
- Who will you select to be part of the study?
- What constraints or ethical issues could your study raise?

Benefits and limitations of action research

One of the benefits of action research in the classroom and other learning situations is that it can address problems and questions in a practical and positive manner with the findings being used directly back in the learning situation. In addition, the teacher/researchers are usually working within their own workplaces and, consequently, can have more ownership and control of the research and monitor its progress. The familiarity with the setting and the teachers and learners can make data collection much easier. There are also considerable benefits for the teacher–learner relationship. Research by Baird and Mitchell (1986) on teacher-research has identified that when teachers and students work together to solve classroom problems, a by-product has often been an increase in student confidence and student willingness to take responsibility for some aspects of what they do as learners. They also report increased levels of student–teacher and student–student collaboration.

In addition to improvements at organizational level action research carried out by practitioners should have an impact on, and inform, education policy. At present this benefit is potential rather than real since at a policy level there seems to be little evidence of ideas percolating up from teachers to policy makers. Hodgson (2010: 4) argues that, 'Policy makers should be interested as part of the whole political and deliberative cycle to work with the views of practitioners and researchers as part of the policy process.'

One of the main limitations of action research is the extra burden and workload that the research project could add to an already demanding job. This may be compounded by funding difficulties which limit the scope of, or prevent, the research. Furthermore, undertaking large projects individually could lead to a sense of isolation and possible criticism from colleagues who do not value what it is you are trying to do. However, if research is supported at a senior managerial level and understood as part of the development of a community of practice with benefits accruing to a wide range of teaching staff, it may become easier to get colleagues on board. Other issues which could limit or constrain the research include ethical considerations and questions of impartiality and confidentiality.

Case studies of action research

Case study 1

The first case study is of research carried out by Jackie H. Jackie is an ESOL lecturer at an FE college. The following is an extract from her initial thoughts on her research

1 **What aspect of teaching and learning ESOL do I want to investigate?**
   The possibilities of increasing lower level ESOL (and possibly low level literacy), learners' ability to work autonomously using ICT.
2 **Why?**
   As ESOL learner numbers decline, and it becomes less profitable to teach ESOL, tutors are asked to teach larger groups of learners of a wider mix of levels. The use of 'roll on roll off' adds to the difficulties of managing such classes.
   Many of the learners I currently teach have often never used a computer, or indeed, experienced formal education.
   Given this situation, and policy moves towards more personalised learning, the tutor is required to focus increasingly on one to one learning for a substantial part of each teaching session.
3 **What would this achieve?**
   It would empower learners with the ability to study independently, both in class and in private study, and to enable the tutor to work with learners as individuals it makes sense that they should be able to self direct their learning without continuous supervision.
4 **What could I do?**
   One way for this to happen is to enable learners – with little ICT knowledge and low levels of English – to work independently using the internet, word processing or ESOL specific software without the need for tutor support to 'get them going'. I want to develop a resource to enable learners with little ICT knowledge and low levels of English to quickly learn how to use, and gain confidence in, word processing, accessing the internet for grammar practice, etc. and using ESOL specific software.
   The research will involve the dissemination of the resource to other tutors to investigate the usefulness of the resource and any areas for improvement or expansion.
5 **Is this feasible in the time**
   Yes if viewed as an initial study.

6 What other support might I need to help with this?
Other ESOL tutors within College.
Literacy tutors?
Peers with greater IT skills than I. IT Department.

Jackie's final report

Project: An ESOL resource to enable independent learning – report

Introduction

In this report I shall explore the background which led to my interest in developing this resource, give a rationale for the project, describe why and how I selected the methodology, discuss my findings and, finally, offer my conclusions as to the effectiveness of the resource and action areas for development.

Setting the scene

In my experience, *effective and appropriate* resources for teaching English for Speakers of Other Languages (ESOL) are not that easy to come by. There are many useful websites with resources that I can, and do, adapt. I attempt to increase my knowledge of different websites and the myriad of resources they offer on a daily basis but this can be time consuming. Finding resources specifically for ESOL/ICT is especially difficult. More often than not I find it less time consuming to create my own resources, tailored to my specific learners and the areas in which they need to develop.

I am, however, limited in my ability to produce high quality and ever-more interesting resources by the limitations of my ICT skills. Enlisting the help of friends and colleagues to increase my skills and giving myself time to practise was essential to producing a good quality resource, I currently teach learners at Entry Level 1, Entry Level 2 and Entry Level 3. For some of the learners I work with this is their first experience of formal education and, for many, this is their first experience of using a computer. Those who have computer skills have basic skills and would certainly, not initially, know the system for accessing the use of computers at the Outreach Centre where I teach.

Rationale

ESOL learner numbers have declined following the withdrawal of automatic *fee* remission from adult ESOL courses up to level 2 and it has become less profitable, if indeed, no longer viable, to teach ESOL within a further education setting. As a result, where ESOL is still taught, tutors are increasingly required to teach larger groups of an increasing mix of levels of learners in order to achieve previous levels of income. I, myself, was, at the beginning of this academic year (September 2008), teaching a maximum of 12 EL1 learners. Currently, I have 15 learners on my register and, as previously stated, ranging through Entry Level 1, 2 and 3.

Government policy is accelerating the pace towards totally personalised learning. Tutors have for some time been using Individual Learning Plans with Individual Targets and are, therefore, focusing increasingly on one to one teaching for a substantial part of each teaching session.

As previously stated, many of the learners I teach have either not used, or have had little experience of using, a computer. A substantial percentage of my learners are diagnosed lower Entry 1 Level and, therefore, have low listening/reading and comprehension skills. One of my current learners displays clear signs of dyslexia although there is no diagnostic test available due to her low levels of English. Added to this, the opportunity for learning support is non-existent because, originally, ESOL class ratios of learners to tutors were said to be set sufficiently low to compensate. However, as I have said, the pressure for tutors to take on more learners in order to secure provision has meant that those low ratios no longer apply in my teaching setting.

To empower learners with the ability to study independently, both in class and in private study, and, therefore, free up the tutor to enable them to work with other learners needing one to one support, it makes sense that learners are more able to self-direct their learning without the need for continuous supervision. It would considerably minimize stress levels for the tutor and clearly develop learners' study skills. It would also encourage learners along the teacher-directed to self-directed learning continuum that Petty refers to which is, for me, a humanistic ideal (Petty, p. 313).

One way for this to happen is to enable learners – with little ICT knowledge and low levels of English – to work independently accessing the Internet and relevant websites for language practice without the need for tutor input to get them started or to 'rescue' them should they accidentally 'de-access' a particular website. It would give learners more confidence to explore the possibilities of ICT, encourage them to further investigate websites and generally motivate learning.

Primary research

I chose to use paper-based questionnaires, separately devised and aimed at learners and tutors, in order to ascertain the effectiveness of the resource. Understanding the differing levels of ICT skill and confidence amongst learners and tutors, and acknowledging the time constraints, not just in the time scale for the research but also upon my fellow tutors (I would be asking for responses during exam time), hard copy, short and easy to complete questionnaires should be sufficient to know whether the resource was going to be of use or not. The next stage was to draft separate questionnaires for tutors and learners, in an attempt to measure the effectiveness of the resource and identify areas for improvement and/or development.

Findings

The process for researching and developing this independent project has thrown up many findings for me both personally and professionally. This has not just arisen from the topic of researching the development and effectiveness of the resource but in the knowledge, skills and experience I have developed along the way.

The profile of the participating learner group was useful to my research. The majority of learners were in the lower levels of English language skills and most had only basic computer skills – clearly a group the resource was aimed at. I didn't expect many learners without any computer skills as we were late in the academic year (keyboard and mouse skills are taught as part of the ESOL courses). The roll on-roll off system that we operate did, however, mean we had two learners who were relatively new and defined themselves as having no computer skills. All other learners self-defined their computer skills as basic or good. The two learners who regarded their computer skills as non-existent, interestingly, differed in their ability to use the resource.

The learners' survey did, however, reveal many useful responses that will enable me to improve and develop the resource. The responses were all very positive and I was left in no doubt as to the usefulness of this as a resource to enable independent learning.

Conclusions

The background to the development of this resource was to produce something for ESOL learners with low levels of English and little experience of using computers that would empower them to begin to work independently.

The theory behind its production was increased learner motivation and an attempt to enable the tutor to work on a more one-to-one basis with learners in a class where numbers have increased and levels have become mixed.

It became clear early on in the process that I would not succeed in producing a resource that could be given to a learner with zero English and zero computer skills and expect them to access the internet without support. I did, however, succeed in producing an effective resource that can be used with some teacher input (initially to give vocabulary, keyboard/mouse practice and a familiarisation of what to expect when using a search engine to access websites) to get learners accessing the internet for grammar practice independently.

Used early on in a scheme of work, or at the beginning of a learner's course the resource should prove a highly effective route to encouraging independent learning, increasing motivation and enabling the tutor to focus on personalised learning in an increasingly difficult setting.

The *proof of the pudding is in the eating* and my learners are now using it every day to remind themselves how to access sites to practise their English grammar. Most of them have repeated the process so often they hardly use it apart from checking that they are using correct spellings, etc. Colleagues have popped into my class to ask to borrow the resource for their learners and my partner (who also teaches Skills for Life) has asked that I make a similar resource for his work setting.

The scope for the improvement and development of the resource is wide. Now that I have acquired the necessary ICT skills to design an illustrative, low-text resource I can cover all the improvement/development areas identified in my findings for use with current and future learners. I can produce resources that enable learners to improve their ICT skills, improve their English skills through online practice and access ESOL specific software. The skills both learners and I have learnt are transferable and will be useful in future settings and situations.

Case study 2

This case study is very appropriate to close this current book, not only because it is a real example of action research and its effectiveness, but because it also includes several key ideas and issues mentioned elsewhere in the book, including: teaching and learning methods; assessment; the use of ICT; reviewing the use of PowerPoint; and the importance of coaching.

Introducing the Tutor Effectiveness Enhancement Programme (TEEP)
(This case study first appeared in LSIS 'Inside Evidence' Spring 2010 Issue 8)

As head of teaching and learning development at Gateshead College, Gillian Forrester set out to introduce 16 staff to TEEP, in order to encourage them to adopt more student-centred practices.

Gillian recognised that her colleagues would need support in doing this so she also used several coaching techniques. To find out the impact of the programme, Gillian ran a structured focus group with 10 of the participants. Personal statements from the tutors showed that the knowledge and skills from the TEEP training programme were successfully transferred into practice by all 16 tutors and that there were many benefits for both the tutors and learners, such as tutors having the confidence to change their practice, greater student engagement and more active involvement in lessons.

What TEEP involves

TEEP draws heavily on research about teaching and learning. The TEEP model is underpinned by a number of strategies relating to assessment for learning, thinking skills, effective use of ICT and collaborative problem-solving. Learners are encouraged to ask their own questions, research their own answers and make use of graphic organisers and mind maps to compare and contrast information. They may be offered a carousel of practical activities (such as making a poster) which all the learners move through, or they can be offered a choice of activities from which they can select. Learners are also given the opportunity to apply what they have learned to other problems, to present their new understanding to others and to defend their views. Fundamental to the approach is the work the tutor does to create an environment conducive to learning. For example, they ensure high challenge and reduce stress by smiling and using 'we' rather than 'you' to refer to the learners and themselves to promote the idea of 'our' learning (i.e. including the tutor's).

The impact TEEP had on the learners

Informal feedback showed Gillian that the learners enjoyed the TEEP lessons hugely compared with previous, more traditional, methods of teaching. The lessons were more fun and engaging due to the use of interactive activities and of resources such as music and video. One tutor who tried to revert back to traditional methods (due to a lack of time) found the learners complained about it being 'the boring way' of learning.

The impact TEEP had on the tutors

The tutors commented on how they had changed to a more student-centred approach. One tutor said, for example, 'Thinking back to my teaching before being introduced to TEEP, my main strategies involved using a lot of PowerPoint presentations in order to get theoretical information across to students'. Another tutor commented: 'I feel I used to run my classes, not exactly with an iron fist, but with an element of control. There were issues with my old methods – primarily that they [the learners] used to regurgitate my handouts/notes'.

Why coaching support was important

The evidence from Gillian's project has led her to believe that the successful introduction of the TEEP programme was due not only to the TEEP approach, but to coaching support too:

- the tutors were organised into pairs to provide each other with support throughout the programme – using video to enable them to reflect on the impact of the new strategies
- a TEEP support group was set up to create a forum to discuss problems and share success stories, and
- the college intranet was used for tutors to share their resources and ideas.

The college had an existing culture that supported open discussion so the tutors were already aware of coaching techniques. This was a great advantage to Gillian and she felt it made all the difference when encouraging the tutors to take on new methods of teaching: 'If you take the coaching element out, it will still be a success, but nowhere near as effective in transferring these skills to actual practice'.

What does Gillian plan to do next?

Gillian found this project to be a phenomenal experience and it's given her lots of evidence for the accreditation in ILN Level 7 qualification. Next she plans to work with TEEP to deliver training for Learning and Skills practitioners. TEEP is already well established in the schools sector, but Gillian feels that practitioners in all phases should be able to develop their practice in this way.

Further reading and sources of information

Bell, J. (2005) *Doing your Research Project*, 4th edn. Maidenhead: Open University Press.
  One of the most popular and accessible introductions to academic research.
Davies, P., Hamilton, M. and James, K. (2007) *Maximising the Impact of Practitioner Re-
  search. A Handbook of Practical Advice*. London: NRDC.
Hamilton, M., Davies, P. and James, K. (2007) *Practitioners Leading Research. A Report
  of Action Research Projects from the NRDC Practitioner-Led Research Initiative (PLRI)*.
  London: NRDC.
Hillier, Y. and Thompson, A. (2005) *Readings in Post-compulsory Education: Research in
  the Learning and Skills Sector*. London: Continuum.
  A good commentary on some of the key ideas about researching in further educa-
  tion with some interesting examples of research.
McNiff, J. (1993) *Teaching as Learning*. London: Routledge.
McNiff, J. and Whitehead, J. (2006) *All you Need to Know about Action Research*. London:
  Sage.
The National Research and Development Centre for Adult Literacy and Numeracy (NRDC)
  As the name suggests, the NRDC specializes in research into teaching and learning
  related to adult skills for life. Even if you are not teaching in this area, it's worth
  looking at their research, both from the point of view of meeting the Minimum
  Core requirements for all teachers, but also to get an insight into research methods.

Websites

British Educational Research Association. http://www.bera.ca.uk/
Educational Evidence Portal. www.eep.ac.uk
LSIS Excellence Gateway *Inside Evidence* research newsletter. Available online at http://
  www.excellencegateway.org.uk/page.aspx?o=195275
LSIS Excellence Gateway *Welcome to research*. http://www.excellencegateway.org.uk/
  page.aspx?o=research
IfL. http://www.ifl.ac.uk/ourvoice/action-research

Bibliography

Armstrong, M. (2003) *A Handbook of Human Resource Management Practice,* 9th edn. London: Kogan Page.

Atkinson, T. and Claxton, G. (eds) (2000) *The Intuitive Practitioner.* Maidenhead: Open University Press.

Avis, J., Fisher, R. and Thompson, R. (eds) (2010) *Teaching in Lifelong Learning: A Guide to Theory and Practice.* Maidenhead: Open University Press.

Baird, J.R. and Mitchell, I.J. (eds) (1986) *Improving the Quality of Teaching and Learning: An Australian Case Study – The PEEL Project.* Melbourne: Monash University.

Bandura, A. (1986) *Social Foundations of Thought and Action.* Englewood Cliffs, NJ: Prentice Hall.

Banks, F. and Shelton Mayes, A. (eds) (2001) *Early Professional Development for Teachers.* Buckingham: Open University Press.

Becta (2007) *British Educational Creativity to All.* Coventry: Becta.

Becta (2009a) *Pushing the Boundaries of Technology: Towards a Future Vision for the Innovative Use of Technology in FE Colleges.* Coventry: Becta.

Becta (2009b) *Our Work, Its Impact.* Coventry: Becta.

Beetham, H. and Sharpe, R. (2007) *Rethinking Pedagogy for a Digital Age.* London: Routledge, Taylor and Francis Group.

Bell, J. (2005) *Doing your Research Project,* 4th edn. Maidenhead: Open University Press.

Berliner, D. (2001) 'Teacher expertise', in F. Banks and A. Shelton Mayes (eds) *Early Professional Development for Teachers.* London: David Fulton Publishers.

Biggs, J. and Tang, C. (2007) *Teaching for Quality Learning at University.* Maidenhead: Open University Press.

Black, P.J. and Wiliam, D. (1998) Assessment and classroom learning. *Assessment in Education,* March: 7–74.

Blakemore, S.-J. and Frith, U. (2005) *The Learning Brain: Lessons for Education.* Oxford: Blackwell.

Blaxter, L., Hughes, C. and Tight, M. (2001) *How to Research,* 2nd edn. Buckingham: Open University Press.

Boud, D., Keogh, R. and Walker, D. (1985) *Reflection: Turning Experience into Learning.* London: Kogan Page.

Brennan, K. (2009) Colleges at the heart of our skills-centric future. Letter to the *Times Educational Supplement,* FE Focus. 13 November.

Brookfield, S. (1995) *Becoming a Critically Reflective Teacher.* San Francisco, CA: Jossey-Bass.

Brookfield, S. (2005) *The Power of Critical Theory for Adult Learning and Teaching.* Maidenhead: Open University Press.

Browne, L., Kelly, J. and Sargent, D. (2008) Change or transformation? A critique of a nationally funded programme of Continuous Professional Development for the Further Education system. *Journal of Further and Higher Education,* 32(4): 427–39.

Burgess, H. (2001) Working with others to develop professional practice, in F. Banks and A. Shelton Mayes (eds) *Early Professional Development for Teachers*. London: David Fulton Publishers.

Burrows, D.E. (1995) The nurse teacher's role in the development of reflective practice. *Nurse Education Today*, 15: 346–50.

Claxton, G. (1999) *Wise Up. Learning to Live the Learning Life*. Stafford: Network Educational Press Limited.

Claxton, G. (2002) *Building Learning Power*. Bristol: TLO Limited.

Claxton, G. and Lucas, B. (2010) *New Kinds of Smart*. Maidenhead: Open University Press.

Coffield, F. (2008) *Just Suppose Teaching and Learning Became the First Priority . . .* London: Learning and Skills Network.

Coffield, F., Moseley, D., Hall, E. and Ecclestone, K. (2004) *Should We be Using Learning Styles?* London: Learning and Skills Research Centre.

Cohen, L., Manion, L. and Morrison, K. (2007) *Research Methods in Education*, 6th edn. London: Routledge.

Cooperrider, D.L. (1990) Positive image, positive action: The affirmative basis of organising, in S. Srivatsva and D.L. Cooperrider (eds) *Appreciative Management and Leadership: The Power of Positive Thought and Action in Organizations* (pp. 91–125). San Francisco: Jossey Bass. (Chapter reprint available at www.stipes.com/aichap2.htm)

Cooperrider, D.L., Whitney, D. and Stavros, J. (2003) *Appreciative Inquiry Handbook*. San Francisco, CA: Berrett-Koehler.

Cousin, G. (2006) An introduction to threshold concepts. *Planet* 17, December. Available at www.gees.ac.uk/planet/p17/gc.pdf (accessed 11 August 2009).

Crawley, J. (2005) *In at the Deep End: A Survival Guide for Teachers in Post Compulsory Education*. London: David Fulton Publishers.

Davison, J. (2008) Why we shouldn't have it all off pat. *Times Educational Supplement*, 14 March.

Day, C. (1999) *Developing Teachers: The Challenges of Lifelong Learning*. London: Routledge.

Deakin Crick, R., Broadfoot, P. and Claxton, G. (2004) Developing an effective lifelong learning: the ELLI project. *Assessment in Education: Principles, Policy and Practice*, 11(3): 247–72.

Denscombe, M. (2007) *The Good Research Guide*. Maidenhead: Open University Press.

Dewey, J. (1933) *How We Think*. New York: D.C. Heath.

DfEE (Department for Education and Employment) (1998) *The Learning Age: A Renaissance for a New Britain*. London: The Stationery Office.

DfEE (Department for Education and Employment) (1999) *A Fresh Start – Improving Literacy and Numeracy. The Report of the Working Group Chaired by Sir Claus Moser*. London: DfEE.

DfES (Department for Education and Skills) (2002) *Success for All: Reforming Further Education and Training*. London: DfES.

DfES (2003) *Subject Specialism: Consultation Document*. London: DfES.

DfES (2004) *Equipping Our Teachers for the Future. Reforming Initial Teacher Training for the Learning and Skills Sector*. London: DfES.

DfES (2006a) *Further Education: Raising Skills, Improving Life Chances.* London: DfES.

DfES (2006b) *Personalising Further Education: Developing a Vision.* London: DfES.

Dweck, C.S. (2006) *Mindset: The New Psychology of Success.* New York: Random House.

Dyck, B. (2009) Me? A teacher-researcher? *Education World.* http://www.educationworld. com/a_curr/voice/voice135.shtml (accessed 25 November 2009).

Ellis, N. (2008) *CPD: A Breakdown, July 2008 issues,* available at: http://www. teachingexpertise.com/articles/cpd-breakdown-4039 (accessed 5 August 2009).

Fairclough, M. (2008) *Supporting Learners in the Lifelong Learning Sector.* Maidenhead: McGraw-Hill.

Fisher, R. (2006) Thinking skills, in J. Arthur, T. Granger and D. Wray (eds) *Learning to Teach in Primary School.* London: Routledge Falmer.

Fisher, R. and Webb, K. (2006) Subject Specialist Pedagogy and initial teacher training for the learning and skills sector in England: the context, a response and some critical issues. *Journal of Further and Higher Education,* 30(4): 337–49.

Forde, C., McMahon, M. and Reeves, J. (2009) *Putting Together Professional Portfolios.* London: Sage Publications.

Foster, A. (2005) *Realising the Potential: A Review of the Future Role of Further Education Colleges.* London: DfES Publications.

Furlong, J. (1998) Educational research: meeting the challenge of change. An inaugural lecture. Graduate School of Education, University of Bristol.

Ganley, B. (2004) Blogging as a dynamic, transformative medium in an American Liberal Arts Classroom, in Thomas N. Burg (ed.) *BlogTalks2* (pp. 295–338). Vienna: Cultural Research.

Gibbs, G. (1988) *Learning by Doing: A Guide to Teaching and Learning Methods.* Oxford: Further Education Unit, Oxford Polytechnic.

Gladwell, M. (2008) *Outliers.* New York: Little Brown.

Gleeson, D. and James, D. (2007) The paradox of professionalism in English Further Education: a TLS project perspective. *Educational Review,* 59(4): 451–67.

Goleman, D. (1995) *Emotional Intelligence.* London: Bloomsbury.

Goleman, D. (1998) *Working with Emotional Intelligence.* London: Bloomsbury.

Guskey, T. (2000) *Evaluating Professional Development.* Thousand Oaks, CA: Corwin Press.

Harkin, J. (2006) Treated like adults: 14–16 year olds in further education, *Research in Post-Compulsory Education,* 11(3): 319–39.

Hart, S., Dixon, A., Drummond, M.J. and McIntyre, D. (2004) *Learning Without Limits.* Maidenhead: Open University Press.

Hayes, D., Marshall, T. and Turner, A. (eds) (2007) *A Lecturer's Guide to Further Education.* Maidenhead: Open University Press.

Hayes, L., Nikolic, V. and Cabaj, H. (2001) *Am I Teaching Well?* Exeter: Learning Matters.

Headley, K. (2009) An investigation into the purpose and value of reflective practice in teacher development in the lifelong learning sector. Unpublished MA dissertation, University of Derby.

Hillier, Y. (2005) *Reflective Teaching in Further and Adult Education,* 2nd edn. London: Continuum.

Hitching, J. (2008) *Professional Development in the Lifelong Learning Sector: Maintaining your Licence to Practise.* Exeter: Learning Matters.

Hodgson, A. (2010) Research in view: interview with Ann Hodgson. *Inside Evidence,* Spring 2010, Issue 8.

Honey, P. and Mumford, A. (1992) *The Manual of Learning Styles.* Maidenhead: Peter Honey Publications.

Hubbard, R.S. and Power, B.M. (2003) *The Art of Classroom Inquiry: A Handbook for Teacher-researchers.* Portsmouth, NH: Heinemann.

IfL (Institute for Learning) (2008a) *Disciplinary Procedure Rules.* London: Institute for Learning.

IfL (2008b) *In Tuition* IfL's member journal, issue 1, Spring.

IfL (2009a) *Guidelines for Your Continuing Professional Development.* London: Institute for Learning.

IfL (2009b) *Professionalism and the Role of Professional Bodies: A Stimulus Paper from the Institute for Learning,* Version 1.0. London: Institute for Learning.

IfL (2009c) *2008–09 IfL Review of CPD: Making a Difference for Teachers, Trainers and Learners.* London: Institute for Learning.

IfL (2009d) *Code of Professional Practice.* London: Institute for Learning.

James, D. and Biesta, G. (2007) *Improving Learning Cultures in Further Education.* London: Routledge.

James, M. and Pollard, A. (2006) *Improving Teaching and Learning in Schools: A Commentary by the Teaching and Learning Research Programme.* London: London University, Institute of Education, TLRP.

Johnson, S. (2006) *Everything Bad is Good for You.* London: Penguin.

Kelly, S. (2006) *The CPD Co-ordinator's Toolkit.* London: Sage Publications.

Kelly, S. (2008) Evaluating the impact of CPD. *CPD Week E-bulletin October 2008.* Available at http://www.teachingexpertise.com/articles/evaluating-impact-cpd-5281 (accessed 25 September 2009).

Kember, D., Ho, A. and Hong, C. (2008) The importance of establishing relevance in motivating student learning. *Active Learning in Higher Education,* 9(3):249–63.

Kennedy, A. (2005) Models of continuing professional development: a framework for analysis. *Journal of In-service Education,* 31(2): 235–50.

Knowles, M.S. (1978) *The Adult Learner: A Neglected Species.* Houston, TX: Gulf Publishing Co.

Kolb, D. (1976) *The Learning Style Inventory.* Boston, MA: McBer.

Kolb, D. (1984) *Experiential Learning – Experience as a Source of Learning and Development.* Englewood Cliffs, NJ: Prentice Hall.

Koschmann, T. (1996) *CSCL: Theory and Practice of an Emerging Paradigm.* Mahwah, NJ: Lawrence Erlbaum Associates.

Land, R., Meyer, J. and Smith, J. (2008) *Threshold Concepts within the Disciplines.* Rotterdam: Sense Publishers.

Lave, J. and Wenger, E. (1990) *Situated Learning: Legitimate Peripheral Participation.* Cambridge: Cambridge University Press.

Lea, J., Hayes, D., Armitage, A., Lomas, L. and Markless, S. (2003) *Working in Post-Compulsory Education.* Maidenhead: Open University Press.

Leitch, S. (2006) *Prosperity for All in the Global Economy: World Class Skills.* London: HM Treasury.

Lifelong Learning UK (2006) *New Overarching Professional Standards for Teachers, Tutors and Trainers in the Lifelong Learning Sector*. London: LLUK.

LSIS (Learning and Skills Improvement Service) Excellence Gateway *Personalisation*. Available at http://www.excellencegateway.org.uk/page.aspx?o=personalisation (accessed 22 November 2009).

Maclean, M. and Mohr, M. (1999) *Teacher-researchers at Work*. Berkeley, CA: National Writing Project.

MacLennan, N. (1995) *Coaching and Mentoring*. Aldershot: Gower Publishing Limited.

Marshall, T. (2007) Educating the digital native, in D. Hayes, A. Marshall, and A. Turner (eds) *A Lecturer's Guide to Further Education*. Maidenhead: Open University Press.

Martin, E. (1999) *Changing Academic Work: Developing the Learning University*. Buckingham: Open University Press.

Martin, M. (2006) Every day a training day, Curriculum Briefing, *Leading Learning, Empowering Teaching*, 4(2). Available at www.teachingexpertise.com/publications/curriculum-briefing-vol-4-no-2-leading-learning-2726 (accessed 13 October 2009).

Marton, F. and Saljo, R. (1976) On qualitative differences in learning 1: outcome and process, *British Journal of Educational Psychology*, 46: 4–11.

McGuinness, C. (1999) *From Thinking Skills to Thinking Classrooms: A Review and Evaluation of Developing Pupils' Thinking*. Nottingham: DfEE.

McMurray, D.W. and Dunlop, M.E. (1999) The collaborative aspects of online learning: a pilot study. Paper originally presented at the 6th International Literacy and Education Research Network Conference, Malaysia, 27–30 September 1999. Available at http://ultibase.rmit.edu.au/Articles/online/mcmurray1.pdf (accessed 6 September 2009).

McNair, S. and Quintero-Re, L. (2008) *CONFINTEA VI United Kingdom National Report: National Report on the Development and State of the Art of Adult Learning and Education (ALE)*. Leicester: NIACE.

McNiff, J. (1993) *Teaching as Learning*. London: Routledge.

McNiff, J. and Whitehead, J. (2006) *All you Need to Know about Action Research*. London: Sage.

Megginson, D. and Whitaker, V. (2003) *Continuing Professional Development*. London: Chartered Institute of Personnel and Development.

Meyer, J. and Land, R. (2003) Threshold Concepts and Troublesome Knowledge: Linkages to Ways of Thinking and Practising within the Disciplines. *ETL Project Occasional Report 4*. Edinburgh: Teaching and Learning Research Project (TLRP).

Mezirow, J. (1991) *Dimensions of Adult Learning*. San Francisco, CA: Jossey-Bass.

Moon, J.A. (2004) *A Handbook of Reflective and Experiential Learning: Theory and Practice*. London: RoutledgeFalmer.

Mortiboys, A. (2005) *Teaching with Emotional Intelligence*. London: Routledge.

Northedge, A. (2003a) Enabling participation in academic discourse. *Teaching in Higher Education*, 8(2): 169–180.

Northedge, A. (2003b) Rethinking teaching in the context of diversity. *Teaching in Higher Education*, 8(1): 17–32.

O'Donnell, A., Hmelo-Silver, C. and Erkens, G. (eds) (2005) *Collaborative Learning, Reasoning and Technology* (Rutgers Invitational Symposium on Education). London: Routledge.

Office for Public Management (OPM) (2008) *Teachers as Innovative Professionals: Report for GTC and the Innovation Unit*. London: OPM. http://www.opm.co.uk (accessed 5 August 2009).

Ofsted (Office for Standards in Education) (2003) *The Initial Training of Further Education Teachers*. London: Ofsted.

Orem, S.l., Binkert, J. and Clancy, A.L. (2007) *Appreciative Coaching: A Positive Process for Change*. New York: John Wiley & Sons Inc.

Pickering, J. (2008) The developmental journey of new teachers in the lifelong learning sector. Unpublished MA dissertation, University of Derby.

Pollard, A. and Trigg, P. (1997) *Reflective Teaching in Secondary Schools*. London: Cassell.

Pollard, A. (ed.) (2002) *Readings for Reflective Teaching*. London: Continuum.

Prensky, M. (2001) Digital natives, digital immigrants. *On the Horizon*, 9(5). Bradford: NCB University Press.

Race, P. (2005) *Making Learning Happen: A Guide for Post-compulsory Education*. London: Sage Publications.

Randle, K. and Brady, N. (1997) Managerialism and professionalism in the 'Cinderella Service'. *Journal of Vocational Education and Training*, 49(1): 121–39.

Reynolds, B. (1965) *Learning and Teaching in the Practice of Social Work*, 2nd edn. New York: Russell and Russell.

Reynolds, B. and Suter, M. (2010) Reflective practice, in J. Avis, R. Fisher, and R. Thompson (eds) *Teaching in Lifelong Learning: A Guide to Theory and Practice*. Maidenhead: Open University Press.

Roam, D. (2008) *The Back of the Napkin: Solving Problems and Selling Ideas with Pictures*. London: Portfolio.

Robson, J. (2006) *Teacher Professionalism in Further and Higher Education*. Oxford: Routledge.

Roffey-Barentsen, J. and Malthouse, R. (2009) *Reflective Practice in the Lifelong Learning Sector*. Exeter: Learning Matters.

Rudduck, J. and Hopkins, D. (1985) Research as a basis for teaching. *Readings from the Work of Lawrence Stenhouse*. London: Heinemann Educational Books.

Ruddock, J. and McIntyre, D. (2007) *Improving Learning Through Consulting Pupils*. London: Routledge.

Saddington, J. (1992) *Learner Experience: A Rich Resource for Learning*, in J. Mulligan and C. Griffin (eds) *Empowerment Through Experiential Learning*. London: Kogan Page.

Scales, P. (2008) *Teaching in the Lifelong Learning Sector*. Maidenhead: Open University Press.

Schön, D. (1983) *The Reflective Practitioner*. New York: Basic Books.

Schön, D. (1987) *Educating the Reflective Practitioner*. San Francisco, CA: Jossey-Bass.

Senge, P.M. (1992) *The Fifth Discipline: The Art and Practice of the Learning Organization*. New York: Doubleday.

Senge, P.M. (1996) The Leader's new work: building learning organizations, in K. Starkey (ed.) *How Organizations Learn*. London: International Thomson Business Press.

Simmons, R. and Thompson, R. (2007) Aiming higher: how will universities respond to changes in initial teacher training for the post-compulsory sector in England? *Journal of Further and Higher Education*, 31(2): 171–82.

Stenhouse, L. (1975) *An Introduction to Curriculum Research and Development*. London: Heinemann.

Sternberg, R.J. (1988) *The Triarchic Mind*. New York: Viking.

Steward, A. (2009) *Continuing Your Professional Development in Lifelong Learning*. London: Continuum.

Stokes, A., King, H. and Libarkin, J. (2007) Research in science education. *Journal of Geoscience Education*, 55(5): 434–8.

Teaching and Learning Research Programme (n.d.) *Neuroscience and Education: Issues and Opportunities*. London: Institute of Education.

Thompson, M. and William, D. (2007) Tight but loose: a conceptual framework for scaling up school reforms, paper presented to American Educational Research Association, Chicago, 9–13 April 2007.

Thomson, A. (2009) Why FE is feeling its age, *Times Educational Supplement*, 2 October.

Training and Development Agency (TDA) (2007) *What Does Good CPD Look Like? TDA Guidelines: Continuing Professional Development*. London: TDA.

Tripp, D. (1993) *Critical Incidents in Teaching*. London: Routledge.

Tufte, E.R. (2006) *The Cognitive Style of PowerPoint: Pitching Out Corrupts Within*. Cheshire, CT: Graphics Press LLC.

Villeneuve-Smith, F., West, C. and Bhinder, B. (2009) *Rethinking Continuing Professional Development in Further Education. Eight Things you Already Know About CPD*. London: Learning and Skills Network.

Wallace, S. (2008) *Teaching, Tutoring and Training in the Lifelong Learning Sector*, 3rd edn. Exeter: Learning Matters.

Wallace, S. and Gravells, J. (2005) *Mentoring in Further Education*. Exeter: Learning Matters.

Wells, G. (1986) *The Meaning Makers*. London: Hodder and Stoughton.

Wenger, E. (1998) *Communities of Practice: Learning, Meaning and Identity*. Cambridge: Cambridge University Press.

Woolfolk, A., Hughes, M. and Walkup, V. (2008) *Psychology in Education*. Harlow: Pearson Education Limited.

Index

abstract concepts zone, 81
Accreditation of Prior Learning (APL)
  SVUK tariff, 23
  towards CTLLS and DTLLS, 22
action research, 10, 47, 49, 65, 93,
  120, 133
  benefits and limitations, 140–1
  case studies, 141–7
  characteristics of, 135
  cycle, 137
  definition of, 134
  ethics, 139–40
  involving learners, 135
  process, 136–8
  'teaching as learning', 134
action research model, of CPD,
  118
active learning, 60, 91, 124, 136
adaptive learning, 14
adult learners, 92, 96
  technology and, 106
advance organizers, 98–9
Advanced Learning Coach (ALC),
  132
androgogy, 92
applied concepts zone, 81
appraisals, 49, 57, 59, 75–7
appreciative coaching, 40, 117
appreciative inquiry, 10, 13–15, 39–40
assessment, 92, 131
  constructive alignment, 92
  for learning, 30, 105
  formative, 51, 99–100
Associate Teacher Learning and Skills
  (ATLS), 19, 20
associate teacher role, differences from
  full teacher role, 21
award-bearing model, of CPD, 17

Back of the Napkin, The, (Roam), 99
Becta (British Educational
  Communications and Technology
  Association), xi, 45, 106, 111,
  112, 148
behaviour management, 105–6, 112
behaviourism, 88–89
Bell, J., 140, 147
Berliner, D. 79, 81
Biesta, G., 12
Black, P.J., 99–100
Blakemore, S-J., 90
Blaxter, L., 139
blogs, 107
Blunkett, D., 95
brain-based learning, 89–90, 108
British Educational Index, 121
British Educational Research Association
  (BERA), 140, 147
Brookfield, S. 39, 40, 148
Building Learning Power, (Claxton), 93–4

cascade model, of CPD, 117
Centres for Excellence in Teacher
  Training (CETTs), 8
Certificate in Teaching in the Lifelong
  Learning Sector (CTLLS), 20, 21, 22,
  30, 73
Chartered Institute of Personal and
  Development (CIPD), 4
Claxton, G. 42, 50, 88
  Building Learning Power, 93–4
coaching
  appreciative, 40, 117
  peer, 62, 119, 124
  subject networks, 125, 132
  teaching and learning technique, 95
coaching-mentoring model, of CPD, 117

Code of Professional Practice, 26, 151
Coffield, F.
  CPD as professional responsibility, 4
  criticism of VAKT, 90
  metaphors of learning, 11
  'poor teachers', 13
collaborative learning, 39
Comberton Village College, CPD case
    study, 64–5
communities of practice, 11, 74, 118
  online discussion boards, use of in, 45
  situated learning and, 90
community of practice model, of CPD,
    118
computer-supported collaborative
    learning (CSCL), 45
concept maps, 98, 109
constructivism, 11, 89, 90
constructivist, 38, 46, 88, 89, 92, 97,
    107, 127
Continuing Professional Development
    (CPD)
  case studies, 64–7
  changing context of, 7–9
  development plan, 56, 57, 61, 63, 68,
      69, 70, 77
  effective, 5, 15, 25, 59, 66
  evaluating CPD events, 61
  measuring the impact of, 67
  models of, 116–8
  paradoxes of, 4–6
  personalized, 10, 25, 63, 121
  process, 53–5
  recording and monitoring, 69–71
  'sheep-dip' approach, 1, 9, 25, 116
Cooperrider, D., 13
critical incident analysis, 38
critical lenses, in reflective practice, 39

deep learning, 89, 91, 97, 98, 102
deficit model, of CPD, 117
Dewey, J. 35–6, 149
digital immigrants, 106

digital natives, 106
Diplomas, 87, 103, 119
  Sector Skills Councils and, 121
  support website, 111
  training for, 132
Diploma in Teaching in the Lifelong
    Learning Sector, 20, 21, 22, 30, 73
Disciplinary Policy, 26–27
dual professionalism,1, 30, 54, 55, 59, 66,
    75, 119
Dweck, C. 49, 50

EBSCO, online journals service, 121
Educational Resources Information
    Centre (ERIC), 121
employability, 100–2, 110
English for speakers of other languages
    (ESOL), 52, 119
  action research case study, 141–9
Equipping Our Teachers for the Future,
    (DfES), 8, 21, 33
evaluation
  action research and, 137
  CPD Impact Evaluation Model,
      67, 68
  evaluation of student performance,
      133
  lesson observation, 47
  peer observation and, 65
Everything Bad is Good for You, (Johnson),
    87
experiential learning, 36, 37, 52, 56

feedback, 30, 37, 38, 42, 48
  developmental, 48, 59, 100
  external, 58
  following observation, 48,
  learner, 42, 57, 100
Fisher, R. 102, 110
formative assessment, 99–100
Foster, A. 17, 101, 150
Foundation degree, 120
Frith, U., 90

full teacher role, difference from full
  teacher role, 21
Functional Skills, 16, 54, 75, 87, 102,
  119, 131
Further Education National Training
  Organisation (FENTO), 18
  standards, 7, 23

generative learning, 14
Gold Dust resources, 11, 108, 110, 111,
  124, 132
Goleman, D., 39, 41
Guskey, T., impact of CPD evaluation
  model, 68

Harkin, J., 105
Honey, P., 37, 90
How We Think, (Dewey), 36
humanism, 89

*Improving Learning Cultures in
  Further Education* (James and
  Biesta), 12
inclusion, 83, 126
Increased Flexibility Programme (IFP),
  105
induction
  case study, 78
  checklist for new teachers, 76
  communities of practice, 80
  experienced 'new' teacher, 74
  new in post, 74, 75
  new teachers, 74
  programme, 75
'informed consent', 139
Initial Learning Plan (ILP)
  personalized learning, 104
  teacher training and, 82
Institute for Leadership and Management
  (ILM), 85
Institute for Learning (IfL), 3, 18, 20, 22,
  24, 25
  Code of Professional Practice, 26, 151

CPD Guidelines, 3, 10, 16, 24, 56, 66,
  67, 87, 121
CPD planning cycle, 56
definition of CPD, 24
disciplinary policy, 26
dual professionalism,1, 54, 75
evaluation model, 68
Impact Evaluation Model, 68
planning cycle, 56
portfolio of evidence, 46
professional dialogue, 11, 119
professionalism, 9, 27, 29, 31
ReFLECT tool, 57, 58, 66, 70, 71
reflective practice, 31, 34, 33, 54, 56,
  58,70
Review of CPD, 9, 151
role in supporting and monitoring
  CPD, 23, 46
role of, 19
strategic aims, 19
suggested CPD activities, 62
support for the, 19
vision, 24
what drives CPD, 55
what is the Ifl?, 18
Integrated Quality and Enhancement
  Review (IQER), 66
internet, use for learning, 106

James, D., 12
Johnson, S., 87

Kelly, S., evaluation of impact of CPD,
  68–9
Knowles, M., 92
Kolb, D., 37, 90, 151

Lave, J. 46, 72, 74, 80, 90
learning
  active 60, 91, 124, 136
  adaptive, 14
  brain-based, 89–90, 108
  collaborative, 39

learning (*Contd.*)
  deep, 89, 91, 97, 98, 102
  effective, 88, 91, 92
  experiential, 36, 37, 52, 56
  generative, 14
  problem-based, 89, 95, 98, 103
  situated, 90
  surface, 89, 97, 98, 109
  transformative, 39
*Learning Age: A Renaissance for a New
  Britain*, (DfES), 95
learning communities, 10, 49,
  74, 138
learning cultures, 12
learning organizations, 5, 14–15, 83
  universities as, 15
Learning Power, four R's of, 93
Learning Power Palette, 94
Learning and Skills Improvement Service
  (LSIS), 16, 85, 104
  Excellence Gateway, 111
  Gold Dust resources, 11, 108, 110, 111,
    124, 132
  Guide to LSIS Services, 16
  STEM (science, technology,
    engineering and mathematics)
    programme, 125, 132
  Subject Learning Coaches, 124
learning styles, 37, 90, 104
  criticism of, 90
learning theory,
  behaviourism, 88
  brain-based, 89
  brief review of, 88
  constructivism, 99
  constructivist, 107, 127
  deep and surface, 89
  humanism, 89
  situated, 92
  social constructivism, 11
  threshold concepts, 128
Leitch, A. 17, 55, 87, 101, 151
lifelong learning, 25, 95–7, 108
  principles, of, 96

Lifelong Learning Sector (LLS), 1, 9, 28,
  31, 50, 59, 84, 96, 117
  LLUK and, 7
  number of people working in, 72
Loughborough College, CPD case study,
  65–7
Lucas, B., 94

managerialism, 1, 7, 10, 12
Martin, M., 14–15
Marton, F., 97
McGuinness, C., 102
McNiff, J., 134, 137
Megginson, D., 4
mental models, in learning
  organizations, 14
mentoring
  new colleagues, 10, 62, 78
  role of, 123
  skills, 123–4
  subject specialist, 114
  subject-specific, 123
Mezirow, J. 38
mindset, 35, 49, 50, 150
Minimum Core, The, 87
Moon, J.A., 39, 44, 52
Mumford, A., 37, 90

National Institute for Adult Continuing
  Education (NIACE), 108
National Occupational Standards (NOSS),
  121
new teachers, 72
  career routes, 83
  communities of practice, 80
  developmental journey of, 78, 81
  induction checklist for, 76
  induction of, 75
  needs of, 73
  'novice to expert', 79
  qualifications, 57, 73
not in education, employment or
  training (NEET), 86
Northedge, A., 127

observations
   being observed, 47–8
   lesson, 60, 66
   peer, 48–9, 65, 95
   teaching and learning, 42, 43, 47
Ofsted, 8, 16, 23, 113
online discussion boards, 45
organizational learning, 5, 15

Personal Development Journals, 43–4
Personal, learning and thinking skills
   (PLTS), 102
personal mastery, in learning
   organizations, 14
plasticity, brain, 90
portfolio of evidence, 46
PowerPoint, using, 107–8
Prensky, M., 106
Preparing to Teach in the Lifelong
   Learning Sector (PTLLS), 19, 20,
   30, 119
problem-based learning, 89, 95,
   98, 103
profession, characteristics of, 26
professional
   definition of, 27
   development, 42, 46, 51, 53, 58, 60, 70
   formation, 22, 23, 30
   identity, 30, 53, 65
   rights and responsibilities of, 29
   values, 28, 30, 32
professionalism, 6, 19, 23, 27, 28, 30, 31,
   53, 66, 77, 134
   decline in, 25
   dual, 30, 54, 55, 59, 66, 75, 119
   LLUK Standards and, 29
   'new', 7
   'paradox of', 31
   three themes of, 27
Professional Practice Committee, 27

QUAD, model of development, 50–1
Qualified Teacher Learning and Skills
   (QTLS), 19, 20, 57

Race, P., 37, 153
reflection, 34
   composite model of, 40
   emotional challenge, 41
   for action, 36
   in action, 36
   on action, 36
   potential barriers to, 41
reflective practice, 36, 37, 44, 46, 51, 56
   action research and, 134
   appreciative inquiry and, 39
   collaborative learning and, 39
   mechanisms for supporting, 42–9
   peer observation and, 48
   transformative learning and , 38
   value of, 34
research
   definition, 138–9
   methodology, 138
Reynolds, B., model of developing
   competence, 79
'ripples on a pond', 37–8
Roam, D., 99
Rogers, C., 89

Saljo, R., 97
scaffolding learning, 92
Schon, D., 36, 37, 153
Science, Technology, Engineering and
   Mathematics (STEM) programme,
   125, 132
Sector Skills Councils (SSCs), 121, 122
self-appraisal, 36
Senge, P., 14, 153
shared vision, in learning organizations,
   15
'Shift Happens', video, 86
Should we be using learning styles,
   (Coffield, et al), 90
situated learning, 90
Skills for Life, 54, 83, 131
Specialist Schools and Academies Trust
   (SSAT), 121
Stenhouse, L., 3, 133, 134

Sternberg, R., 50
subject associations, TDA list of, 128–31
Subject Learning Coaches (SLCs), 124–5, 132
subject specialism, 6, 24, 75, 113
    auditing own subject knowledge and skills, 116
    'mapping the territory', 114–5
    relevance to students, 127–8
    selling your subject', 125–6
subject-specific CPD activities
    examiner, assessor and verifier roles, 119
    gaining qualifications, 119
    giving presentations, 120
    industrial updating, 119
    reading, 120
    working with awarding bodies, 120
    writing, 120
subject-specific mentoring, 123–4
Success for All (DfES), 8
surface learning, 89, 97, 98, 109
SVUK (Standards Verification UK), 23
systems thinking, in learning organizations, 15

tacit knowledge, 36, 40
Teacher Development Agency (TDA)
    effective CPD, model of, 59–61
    Establishing a Culture of Continuing Professional development Engagement, 70
    list of subject associations, 129–30
    professionalism, view of, 29
teacher experience zone, 81
Teaching and Learning Research Project (TLRP)
    personalised learning, 111
    ten principles of effective learning, 91–3

teaching and learning techniques, developing, 95
team learning, in learning organizations, 15
technical rationality, 36
technology,
    collaborative learning and, 45
    LLUK Application Guides, 112
    online discussion boards, 45
    PowerPoint, 107–8
    role of teacher, impact on, 106
    social exclusion and, 106
    using, 106, 112
'theory-builders', teachers as, 11
thinking skills, 87, 102, 103, 110, 114, 128, 136
training model, of CPD, 117
transformative learning, 38
transformative model, of CPD, 118
Tripp, D., critical incident analysis, 38–9
Tufte, E., 107
Tutor Effectiveness Enhancement Programme (TEEP), action research case study, 145–7

UK Commission for Employment and Skills (UKCES), 121
University of Derby, 45, 73

VAKT, xii, 90, 91
Villeneuve-Smith, 9, 25, 110
Vygotsky, L., 89

Wells, G., 11, 97
Wenger, E., 46, 72, 74, 80, 90
Whitaker, V., 4
Whitehead, J., 134
wikis, 107
William, D., 99–100

SUPPORTING LEARNERS IN THE LIFELONG LEARNING SECTOR

Marilyn Fairclough

978-0-335-23362-5 (Paperback)
2008

eBook also available

Supporting Learners
in the Lifelong Learning Sector

Marilyn Fairclough

This is the first book of its kind to deal with the topic of *supporting* learners in PCET, rather than just focusing on how to teach them.

Key features:

- Each chapter cross-referenced to the QTLS Professional Standard for those on PTLLS, CTLLS and DTLLS courses
- Real life examples from a variety of settings and subjects
- Practical suggestions for developing classroom practice
- Suggestions for managing disruptive behaviour

www.openup.co.uk

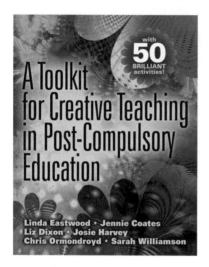

A TOOLKIT FOR CREATIVE TEACHING IN POST-COMPULSORY EDUCATION

Linda Eastwood, Jennie Coates, Liz Dixon, Josie Harvey, Chris Ormondroyd and Sarah Williamson

978-0-335-23416-5 (Paperback)
2009

eBook also available

This is the essential resource for trainees and teachers working in the PCET sector who are looking for new and creative ways of engaging and motivating their learners.

Key features:

- 50 practical and innovative teaching activities
- Variations and subject-specific examples
- Thinking Points to encourage reflection
- A theoretical framework which sets the activities within the context of creativity and innovation

www.openup.co.uk

 OPEN UNIVERSITY PRESS
McGraw · Hill Education

**CONTEMPORARY ISSUES IN
LIFELONG LEARNING**

**Vicky Duckworth and
Jonathan Tummons**

978-0-335-24112-5 (Paperback)
October 2010

This book provides an up-to-date and critical analysis of contemporary issues and debates in the lifelong learning sector (LLS). The authors examine significant issues in the LLS today including inclusive practice, the employability agenda, the curriculum in the LLS and research-led teaching.

There are practical strategies and reflective tasks that encourage readers to become critical, questioning practitioners. Other helpful features include:

- Learning outcomes at the beginning of each chapter
- Links to QTLS standards
- Case studies
- End of chapter summaries
- Further reading and useful websites

www.openup.co.uk

OPEN UNIVERSITY PRESS
McGraw · Hill Education